MW01248229

Where Do I Belong?

Finding Our True Home
Through the Study of Exile in the Bible

Written by Dr. Joel Muddamalle, Melissa Spoelstra and Jenny Wheeler
Designed by Morgan Broom | Copyright ©2024 by Proverbs 31 Ministries
All Scripture quotations are Christian Standard Bible (CSB) unless otherwise noted.

EXILE IN THE BIBLE WAS OFTEN *lonely* ... BUT WE DON'T HAVE TO STUDY IT *alone!*

For a small-group experience, grab a few of your go-to Bible study gals, church community group, neighbors or friends, and plan to gather once a week to discuss what you're learning throughout this study. We've even created **"Where Do I Belong? A Small Group Discussion Guide"** to provide conversation topics, questions and prompts that make it easy for your group to gather and grow together. Scan the QR code to download this **free** group resource!

PAIR YOUR STUDY GUIDE WITH THE FIRST 5 MOBILE APP!

This study guide is designed to accompany your study of Scripture in the First 5 mobile app. You can use it as a standalone study or as an accompanying guide to the daily content within First 5. First 5 is a free mobile app developed by Proverbs 31 Ministries to transform your daily time with God.

Go to the app store on your smartphone, download the First 5 app, and create a free account!
WWW.FIRST5.ORG

Hi, *friend,*

Joel here. As we start this journey of *Finding Our True Home Through the Study of Exile in the Bible* ... I remember when I was 11 years old and my parents sold their house. They told us we were going to move to a different city 45 minutes away. In those few minutes, my world felt like it was falling apart in front of my eyes.

I instantly began to think about everything that was going to change, everything I was going to lose:

- My room, filled with my favorite posters, toys and things I'd collected over the years.
- My garage, where my bike was parked so I could grab it to go ride the block, checking to see if my friends were outside to play.
- My friends!
- My twin brother and sister's room next door, where I could hear them crying in their cribs at night. (Yes, the crying was annoying, but it reminded me they were close. I guess their cries were like my sound machine at night that put me right to sleep. In our new place, their room would be on the other side of the house, and I knew the silence would feel deafening.)

All the familiarity of what I knew to be "home" was gone when we moved into a new house, and everything felt out of place and uncomfortable. Even the block felt wrong to me. And my mind would often wander in those early years ... back to what I considered my **real home.**

Have you ever been homesick? Maybe it was when you moved from one city to another. Or maybe it wasn't a move but a family change. Or a job change. Or the loss of someone close to you, someone you always associated with safety and comfort. Whatever losses or changes you've experienced in your life, you've probably felt the sadness, anxiousness and longing of homesickness: a desire to return to how things were before or how things should be.

The Bible is actually filled with people who felt homesick too. The story of

Scripture starts with God creating a beautiful garden, which was intended to be a home for humanity. But humans chose sin — which created a forceful separation between us and our Father God, removing us from our original home. In other words, humans were *exiled* from the garden. And we still experience this exile today. We sometimes feel out of place, living in a world broken by sin. We long for a safe place to settle down when life feels so unsettling. We long for a loving family that makes us feel valued and included. We long for a restored relationship with God.

As we'll see, these feelings and consequences of exile play a massive thematic role throughout the story of Scripture. In our study, we will explore the theme of exile in both the Old and New Testaments by looking at 30 key examples of how God's people navigated seasons of displacement, disorientation and wilderness wandering. And maybe surprisingly, what we'll find is that there has always been persistent hope for God's people even in exile. In the midst of exile, God's people learn discipline. They learn the importance of preparation. They are positioned to become evangelists Ultimately, they are prompted to glorify God.

Exile is hard — there's no doubt about it. But every hard moment of our lives is laced with hope. Because no matter how lost we may feel in the wilderness of this world, God has sent a Savior to end our exile forever: Jesus. For all who trust in Him, His return will one day usher in our eternal homecoming to a new heaven and new earth.

So let's dig in together and find out what His Word says about our **real home** — where we truly belong.

—*Joel, Melissa and Jenny*

A 30,000-FOOT VIEW *of* EXILE: HOW DID IT *Start,* AND HOW WILL IT *End?*

Every now and then, you might watch a movie that starts with a sneak peek of the ending to help set up the story. Let's start our study of the biblical theme of exile the same way: with the end in mind.

The last book of the Bible, Revelation, gives us prophetic glimpses of a future time when Jesus will return to gather all who believe in Him and bring us home to dwell with God forever:

*"Then I saw **a new heaven and a new earth**; for the first heaven and the first earth had passed away, and the sea was no more. I also saw the holy city, the **new Jerusalem**, coming down out of heaven from God, prepared like a bride adorned for her husband"* (Revelation 21:1-2, emphases added).

*"Then he showed me the river of the water of life, clear as crystal, flowing from the throne of God and of the Lamb down the middle of the city's main street. The **tree of life** was on each side of the river, **bearing twelve kinds of fruit**, producing its fruit every month. **The leaves of the tree are for healing** the nations, and **there will no longer be any curse**. The throne of God and of the Lamb will be in the city, and his servants will worship him. They will see his face, and his name will be on their foreheads"* (Revelation 22:1-4, emphases added).

What a beautiful vision of the end of exile. If we pay close attention to the details of Revelation 21:1, we find a connection between the earthly and heavenly: A *"new heaven and a new earth"* will come into existence as the final establishment of our future home. And the details of Revelation 22:1-4 indicate that the *"new Jerusalem"* is in fact a return and a redemption of the garden of Eden, now transformed into a majestic city filled with God's presence and His family. What a joy to imagine what our homecoming will look like in this place!

But now, with the end in mind, we are faced with the reality of why Revelation 21:1 says *"the first heaven and the first* earth" must "pa[ss] away." In Genesis 1-2, God created all things, both spiritual and earthly, and all He created was good. But tragically, in Genesis 3, both a spiritual and earthly rebellion took place and fractured all of creation. The serpent, Satan, sinned in his rebellion against God (Luke 10:18), and Adam and Eve followed the suggestion of the serpent to also disobey God. This set into motion a type of exile for all humanity that is both spiritual and earthly. Adam and Eve were separated physically from God as a byproduct of their spiritual separation from God ... and our sin separates us from God too.

This explains why Revelation 22:3 says *"there will no longer be any curse"* in the new heaven and the new earth: In our current earthly reality, everything is tainted by the curse of sin and death that entered the world in Genesis 3. Humankind is far from home — far from God — and the longer our sin abounds, the further away we drift. Words like "exile," "wilderness," "sojourning" and "strangers/estrangement" are all ways of describing this state of being and showing the separation between people and God.

But there is good news. While we were far from Him, Jesus came near to us as God in human form and died on the cross to bridge the gap and reconnect humanity to the Father. When we place our faith in Jesus, our spiritual exile ends, even though we will continue living in the tension of our earthly exile until God brings us home with Him. We are spiritually reunited with the Father through the indwelling Holy Spirit today (Ephesians 1:13), and we await the ultimate promised reunion that is on its way tomorrow for all children of God.

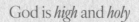

God is *high* and *holy*

Past

GOD AND HUMANITY
DWELLED TOGETHER

MOUNTAIN OF GOD:
EDEN

Increasing sin caused
increasing separation
between people and God

The first sin broke our
relationship with God

A holy, good Father can't
dwell with sinful children

*"through one man's disobedience
the many were made sinners ...
sin multiplied ..."*

ROMANS 5:19-20

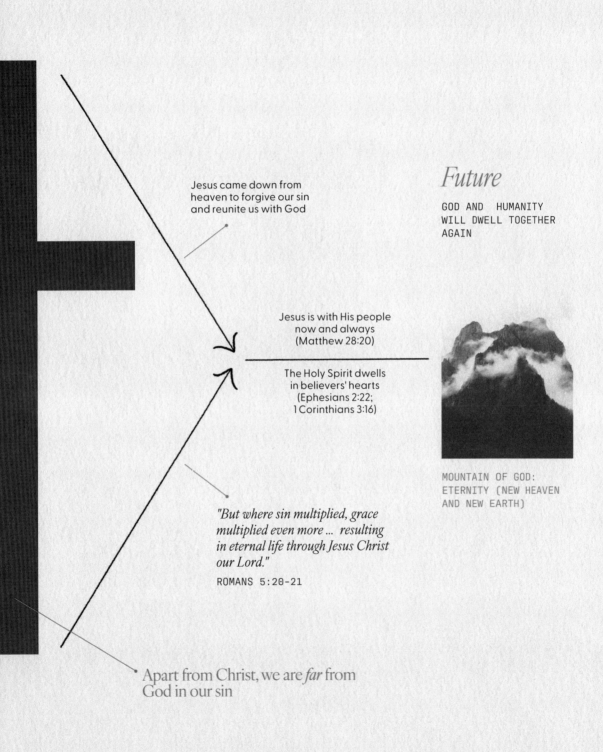

Jesus came down from
heaven to forgive our sin
and reunite us with God

Future

GOD AND HUMANITY
WILL DWELL TOGETHER
AGAIN

Jesus is with His people
now and always
(Matthew 28:20)

The Holy Spirit dwells
in believers' hearts
(Ephesians 2:22;
1 Corinthians 3:16)

MOUNTAIN OF GOD:
ETERNITY (NEW HEAVEN
AND NEW EARTH)

*"But where sin multiplied, grace
multiplied even more ... resulting
in eternal life through Jesus Christ
our Lord."*

ROMANS 5:20-21

Apart from Christ, we are *far* from
God in our sin

IMPORTANT *Terms* RELATED TO EXILE: OLD TESTAMENT AND NEW TESTAMENT

Throughout the Bible, we find the theme of exile both explicitly and implicitly. Explicitly, some scriptures literally use words meaning "exile," whether in Hebrew (in the Old Testament) or Greek (in the New Testament). "Exile" foundationally means "to be away from one's homeland."

Implicitly, there are some related words and images that also convey exilic ideas, such as "wilderness," "wandering," "sojourners," "strangers" or "scattering." The entire book of Exodus, for instance, does not actually use the word "exile," yet it shows us an experience of exile in the lives of God's people when they were on the run, fleeing a land of slavery and searching for a homeland promised by God. Books of the Bible like Daniel and Esther also present individuals who were living in the context of exile during times when God's people were forcibly removed from their homeland.

As we study the theme of exile, here are a few key terms we will discover and some examples of their usage in Scripture.

OLD TESTAMENT *(Hebrew)* WORDS:

Gālâ: A verb meaning "to reveal, uncover, remove, go away, go into exile, be in exile."[1]
- *"On the twenty-seventh day of the twelfth month of the thirty-seventh year of the exile [gālâ] of Judah's King Jehoiachin …"* (2 Kings 25:27).
- *"The Israelites who had returned from exile [gālâ] ate it, together …"* (Ezra 6:21).
- *"He will rebuild my city, and set my exiles* [gālâ] *free …"* (Isaiah 45:13b).

Zārâ: A verb meaning "to scatter, winnow, disperse." (Note: Winnowing was a step in the ancient harvesting process that involved separating the usable from the unusable parts of the grain.)
- *"But I will scatter [zārâ] you among the nations … So your land will become desolate, and your cities will become ruins"* (Leviticus 26:33).

Nādaḥ: A verb meaning "to impel, banish, thrust."
- *"When all these things happen to you—the blessings and curses I have set before you—and you come to your senses while you are in all the nations where the Lᴏʀᴅ your God has driven you [nādaḥ] …"* (Deuteronomy 30:1).

NEW TESTAMENT *(Greek)* WORDS:

Diaspora: A noun meaning "dispersion" (in Scripture, usually referring to Jews who lived outside of the promised land/homeland of Israel).
- *"… To those chosen, living as exiles dispersed abroad [diaspora] in Pontus, Galatia, Cappadocia, Asia, and Bithynia …"* (1 Peter 1:1).
- *"… To the twelve tribes dispersed abroad [diaspora]. Greetings"* (James 1:1).

Skorpizō: A verb meaning "to scatter, disperse." (Note: Jesus refers to those who come against Him and the Kingdom of God as trying to "scatter" God's people, but Jesus is the Good Shepherd who will not allow His sheep to be "scattered.")
- *"I am the good shepherd. The good shepherd lays down his life for the sheep … The wolf then snatches and scatters [skorpizō] them"* (John 10:11-12).

Metoikizō: A verb meaning "to deport, resettle." The noun form, **metoikesia**, also means "forced emigration, deportation." (Note: This translates directly to "exile" and is the word most often used as an equivalent for the Hebrew word *gālâ*.)
- *"You took up … the images that you made to worship. So I will send you into exile [metoikiō] beyond Babylon"* (Acts 7:43).
- *"And Josiah fathered Jeconiah and his brothers at the time of the exile [metoikesias] to Babylon. After the exile [metoikesian] to Babylon Jeconiah fathered Shealtiel …"* (Matthew 1:11-12).

---

[1]Benjamin M. Austin and Jonathan Sutter, "Exile," *Lexham Theological Wordbook*, Lexham Bible Reference Series, ed. Douglas Mangum et al. (Bellingham, WA: Lexham Press, 2014).

Eras OF EXILE IN BIBLICAL HISTORY

Another way to break down the theme of exile in Scripture is to look at different time periods chronologically. Though this is not a comprehensive outline, below are some of the most important eras of exile in the Bible.

Some exiles are more personal (one person or family being banished, scattered, sent into the wilderness) while other exiles are corporate (for instance, the national exile of Israel or the exile of all humankind due to sin). Throughout our study, we'll also consider how we have all experienced "exile eras" in our own lives and how our experiences fit into this larger story of God's people across history.

Adam and Eve's exile from the *garden*
GENESIS 3

Adam and Eve were sent out of their home, Eden, as a consequence of sin. This set in motion the larger exile of all sinful humanity being sent away from home, or separated from God.

Cain's exile
GENESIS 4

Cain followed the path of his parents' (Adam and Eve's) sins. As a consequence, he was separated from his family and from the Lord's presence.

Noah's exile on the *ark*
GENESIS 7

Sin spread throughout the world, and God sent Noah and his family into a type of temporary exile on the ark while the world was flooded — but they were saved through this exile, and God re-created the world.

Exile at *Babel*
GENESIS 11

Sin continued; the families of the world rebelled against God by pridefully constructing a tower. As a consequence, the unity they once had was dismantled when God mixed up their languages and scattered them across the world.

(Circa 2166-1925 B.C.)* *Abraham's* exile
GENESIS 12

God called Abraham to leave his family and homeland to follow God to a new promised land. God would bless the world through Abraham's family, which became the nation of Israel.

(Circa 1929-1785 B.C.)* *Jacob's* exile
GENESIS 27

Jacob tricked his brother Esau in order to steal his birthright. As a consequence, Jacob was cast out of his family and sent away from home, though God later redemptively brought him back.

(Circa 1900-1700 B.C.)* *Joseph's* exile
GENESIS 37

Jacob's son Joseph was captured by his brothers and sold into exile and captivity in Egypt. But God ultimately raised Joseph to a position of power and brought Joseph's family (the Israelites) to Egypt.

(Circa 1859-1688 B.C.)* Israel's exile in *Egypt*
EXODUS 1

The Israelites were fruitful in Egypt, but eventually they were enslaved as captives in a land not their own.

(Circa 1486-1315 B.C.)* *Moses'* exile
EXODUS 2

Moses sinned by killing an Egyptian. As a consequence, he went into exile. Yet in exile, Moses met God, who called him to lead Israel out of Egypt.

(Circa 1446-1234 B.C.)* Israel's *wilderness* wandering
NUMBERS 14

What should have been a short journey from Egypt to the promised land turned into 40 years of wandering in the wilderness, and an entire generation died in exile due to their sin. However, in time, God delivered His people into the homeland He had promised.

(Circa 1025-1000 B.C.)* King *David's* exile
1 SAMUEL 21-23

David was a leader of Israel long after Moses. He left his family to be adopted into the household of Saul, Israel's first king. But when God said David would become the next king, Saul tried to kill him, and David found himself exiled in the wilderness for a time, until God's promise came true.

(Circa 905-930 B.C.)* Exile within *Israel*
1 KINGS 12

The kingdom of Israel, once united under David's rule, went through civil war, and the household of David was broken into two. God's people were divided and exiled/scattered into fractured parts.

(722 B.C.) Israel's exile in *Assyria*
2 KINGS 16-17

The northern kingdom of Israel was conquered by Assyria and went into exile as God's judgment for their sins.

(586 B.C.) Judah's exile in *Babylon*

2 KINGS 25

Often simply called "The Exile": The southern kingdom of Judah fell to Babylon, and the people went into exile as God's judgment for their sins. Still, God would deliver His people out of exile when they repented.

(Circa 444-6 B.C.)* God's *silence*

After Israel's prophets ceased speaking – during the timespan from Nehemiah to the birth of Jesus – came a time often called the "400 years of silence." This may have been part of the famine of the Word of God prophesied in Amos 8:11.

(Circa 6 B.C.-30 A.D.)* *Jesus'* exile/incarnation

Jesus both embodied and redeemed various kinds of exile in His life, ministry, death, resurrection and ascension.

(Circa 30 A.D.-present day)* The *Church's* exile

Though believers in Jesus are no longer spiritually exiled from God, the Apostles and the early Church experienced other kinds of exile as believers in an unbelieving world, which is still true of Christians today.

Note about dates: These date ranges are approximations. Since Scripture does not give us exact dates, these are educated guesses by scholars. The dates listed include possible early and late dates of these events ("circa" meaning "around"), adapted from Faithlife's Logos Bible Study Software timelines.

THE PEOPLE IN EXILE:
God's Design for Diaspora

As we've already discussed, we will sometimes come across the word "diaspora" in reference to the people of God as we study exile in the Bible. This is an important word for us as Christians to understand today. Throughout the Bible and in Jewish history and writings, the word "diaspora" often describes the people of God who did not return to their homeland (Israel) after the Babylonian exile.

The actual Greek word "diaspora" – often translated in English as "dispersion" or "dispersed" – appears three times in the New Testament (John 7:35; James 1:1; 1 Peter 1:1). But the concept and basic ideology is found throughout the Bible. As we look at the idea of diaspora, we ultimately discover that God's people have always had a place and purpose in the world, even if they were scattered in places that were not their home.

We see this clearly in scriptures like Jeremiah 29:5-7, where God commanded His people to do the following things during their exile in Babylon:

- *"Build houses and live in them."*
- *"Plant gardens and eat their produce."*
- *"Find wives for yourselves, and have sons and daughters. Find wives for your sons and give your daughters to men in marriage so that they may bear sons and daughters. Multiply there; do not decrease."*
- *"Pursue the well-being of the city I have deported you to. Pray to the Lord on its behalf, for when it thrives, you will thrive."*

Though Babylon wasn't their homeland, God enabled His people to thrive in the diaspora – sustaining themselves physically (building, planting and eating); socially (marrying and starting families); and spiritually (praying). They were called to maintain their core identity as God's people yet also *"pursue the well-being of the city"* (Jeremiah 29:7) and minister to others around them.

It's interesting to note that the word "diaspora" was associated "nearly exclusively [with] the Jewish people until the 1970s."[2] But today, it's also used in more general references to people or groups who are living outside of their homeland. In some cases, the place of exile or diaspora becomes a type of home for a season or even for generations.

This concept of diaspora is vitally important to us as believers in Jesus today, as we (the modern Church) live in the reality of exile. We are sojourners and strangers in a land that is not our own as we await the return of our King, Jesus, who will bring with Him the fullness of His Kingdom. In the meantime, our "exile" on earth is in fact an opportunity to establish outposts of the heavenly Kingdom of God. Wherever God's people gather, serve and live in faithfulness to Him, God's Kingdom is established as a beacon of hope for a hurting world.

[2]Scott R. Moore, "Diaspora," *The Lexham Bible Dictionary*, ed. John D. Barry et al. (Bellingham, WA: Lexham Press, 2016).

WHAT YOU HAVE TO LOOK
Forward TO IN THIS STUDY

DAILY TEACHINGS AND REFLECTION QUESTIONS

Each day of this study teaches on a key Scripture passage related to the biblical theme of exile, unwrapping God's Word and helping us understand how to apply it to our lives. Throughout the teachings, you'll also find reflection questions to guide your personal study.

BONUS PAGES

Sprinkled throughout this guide are supplementary charts, maps, timelines, Hebrew and Greek word studies, illustrations, and other bonus pages that will also help you dig deeper into the details and context of God's Word.

WEEKEND VIDEOS AND PRAYERS

Each week of this study concludes with a special video teaching that will provide additional insight and answer important questions about what we've learned that week. You'll access the videos via QR codes printed right here in this study guide — don't miss the chance to hear from Proverbs 31 Ministries writers, staff members and professional Bible scholars who each have a unique message to share about the theme of exile in Scripture! Finally, we'll close every week together with a guided prayer.

OPTIONAL SMALL GROUP RESOURCE

Exile in the Bible was often lonely ... but we don't have to study it alone! For a small-group experience, grab a few of your go-to Bible study gals, church community group, neighbors or friends, and plan to meet once a week to discuss what you're learning throughout this study. We've even created "Where Do I Belong? A Small Group Discussion Guide" to provide conversation topics, questions and prompts that make it easy for your group to gather and grow together. Scan the QR code at the very front of this book or visit https://first5.org/video-study to download this free group resource!

Major MOMENTS

WEEK 1: HOW DID WE GET *So Far* FROM *Home?*

GENESIS 1-2
God brought order to chaos to establish His peace in the home He created for humanity.

GENESIS 3
Adam and Eve sinned, and all humanity was exiled as a result.

GENESIS 4:1-16
God is a God of compassion and provided protection and care even in the midst of Cain's exile.

GENESIS 6-8
God used a type of exile to save Noah and his family from the flood.

GENESIS 11:1-9
The pride of humanity led to ruin and exile at Babel.

WEEK 2: WHERE IS *God* IN OUR EXILE?

GENESIS 12:1-3; GENESIS 16:1-12; GENESIS 21:8-19
God is committed to having His family back together and chose one family to be a blessing to all the nations of the world.

GENESIS 27; GENESIS 39:1-23
Sin led Jacob and Joseph into exile, but God's grace led them through it and back to His plan for their lives.

EXODUS 1:1-14; EXODUS 3:7-10
Even in their exile, God saw, heard and knew about His people's affliction and acted to bring about their rescue.

NUMBERS 13-14
Because God's people disobeyed Him, they were sent to wander in the wilderness for 40 years.

JUDGES 2:11-15; JUDGES 17:6
When Israel rejected and neglected God as King, the consequence was self-imposed exile.

WEEK 3: WHO CAN *End* OUR EXILE?

1 SAMUEL 22:1-2; 1 KINGS 12
Israel and Judah divided into two separate kingdoms.

1 KINGS 19:1-8
Elijah rested after he encountered rejection.

2 KINGS 17:1-23
Assyria conquered and exiled Israel.

2 KINGS 25:1-21
Babylon conquered and exiled Judah.

MALACHI 4:4-6
During 400 years of silence, God's people did not hear new revelation from Him.

WEEK 4: HOW DID *Jesus* EXPERIENCE EXILE?

JOHN 1:1-14
Jesus holds the world together, but the world did not recognize Him.

MATTHEW 2:13-21
As a child, Jesus escaped to Egypt for safety, though He would later return home to Israel.

MATTHEW 4:1-11
Jesus was tempted in the wilderness and was faithful and obedient to God.

MATTHEW 27:45-46; PSALM 22:1
In His human nature, Jesus experienced true and total exile on the cross.

ACTS 1:4-11
Jesus returned home to heaven and took His rightful place at the right hand of the Father.

WEEK 5: HOW DO WE FIND *Community* IN EXILE?

ACTS 2
Pentecost reunited exiles and launched the Church.

ACTS 15:1-20
The early Church gathered, addressed conflict, and established principles for unity during the Council at Jerusalem.

HEBREWS 10:22-25
The exiles were instructed to gather and were taught how to live while facing persecution.

1 PETER 2:11-17
Exiled Christians learned what it meant to live honorably and humbly within the community and before others.

MATTHEW 28:18-20; 2 CORINTHIANS 5:18-20
Jesus commanded His disciples to spread the message of salvation and reconciliation to God.

WEEK SIX: WHERE IS OUR *True Home?*

EPHESIANS 1:1-14
The Holy Spirit is the first installment of the Christian's inheritance.

PSALM 90
God's people find their home in God's presence rather than a place.

2 PETER 3:1-13
Peter called believers to live holy lives as we wait for the new heaven and the new earth.

HEBREWS 4
God offers rest to His people.

REVELATION 21
A new heaven and a new earth will mark the end of exile.

how did we
ge........
home?

WEEK (One)

HOW DID WE GET SO FAR FROM HOME?

WEEK ONE

The beginning of a story is important to understanding how the rest of the story unfolds.

This is especially true of the story of humanity. Our story begins with a good God, who created good things. In Genesis 1 and 2, we find that God, the perfect Father, Son and Holy Spirit, created the world. After each of His seven creative acts in Genesis 1, Scripture summarizes that God's actions were *"good."* But the one thing that was the *"very good"* (Genesis 1:31) epitome of creation, the crown jewel, was humanity, starting with Adam and Eve.

One specific biblical detail that reinforces the idea of God as a good Father to humanity is in Genesis 1:26-27, which says Adam and Eve were created in God's *"likeness"* and *"image."* We're going to get into this more on Day 2 of this week's study, but just as a teaser, the Hebrew words for "likeness" and "image" were often used in Ancient Near Eastern literature to describe the relationship between a king and his children.

The details here are worth exploring as we start our study of exile in the Bible — because the story of humanity didn't start in exile. It started in Eden. God created Eden as a home for His royal children, and there God interacted,

walked and talked with Adam and Eve (Genesis 3:8). Eden was humanity's first home, where people lived in the presence of God, which gave them both comfort and confidence.

Home is intended to be a place of safety, security, pleasure and joy.

Home should be the place where our hearts feel at rest.

Home should be the place where we can be exactly who we are, without any hiding or pretense.

Ideally, at home, it's OK to be vulnerable. The English word "vulnerable" actually comes from the Latin word *vulnerare*, which means "to wound." But Eden was such a special home because it was a place where Adam and Eve could be truly vulnerable *without fear* of being wounded by God, their Father and Protector (Psalm 46:1; Proverbs 18:10; 2 Thessalonians 3:3).

But while they didn't have to fear wounding from God, tragically, they were tempted to wound themselves. And that is exactly what took place. In Genesis 3, the serpent tempted Eve to eat from the tree of the knowledge of good and evil, which God had forbidden. At the core of the temptation were questions designed to breed doubt: Is God actually a good Father? Is God withholding something from His children out of cruelty and selfishness?

Eve, along with Adam, looked at the fruit, saw that it was pleasant, then took it and ate it (Genesis 3:6). Notice the pattern here:

1. They **saw** that the fruit looked good.

2. They **reached** to take for themselves something that did not belong to them.

3. They **ate** the fruit and enjoyed its momentary pleasure.

These actions were physical in nature, but they had spiritual ramifications. Let's take a look at this pattern again with both a physical and spiritual context in place:

1. They **saw** with their physical eyes how pleasant the fruit was. But pride blinded their spiritual eyes to the blatant temptation to distrust God.

2. They **reached** with their hands to take what they thought would make them *"like God"* (Genesis 3:5), but in doing so, they spiritually rebelled *against God*.

3. They **ate** the fruit and enjoyed its pleasure in the moment, but they also experienced death. This set into motion their eventual physical deaths as well as bringing the spiritual death of sin into the world.

What exactly is exile? It is to be separated from home. And what makes a home? The people or family within the home. So Adam and Eve were sent into exile because they chose to leave the safety of God's family to pursue sin. And this sets the stage for the story of humanity: We were once safe at home, but because of our sin, we've entered into wandering in the wilderness.

Exile is anything but safe and secure. In exile, we may feel anxious, lonely, fearful, confused and definitely homesick. But, friend, there is such good news for us: God is still a good Father even in the midst of our sin and rebellion. And God is set on having His family back together. He wants to rescue us from our exile and help us return home.

That's what we will look at this week. We will work through Genesis 1-11, the opening chapters of the Bible, and see how the theme of exile frames the story of God's children. Specifically, we will learn to train our eyes to look beyond and through the devastation of exile to see the beauty and purpose that can be found even in this very hard reality.

— *Dr. Joel Muddamalle*

day 1 / GENESIS 1-2

God brought order to chaos to establish His peace in the home He created for humanity.

Everyone has a pet peeve, some kind of annoyance that absolutely undoes them. For me, it's disorder. When I walk into my home office and realize my kids have gotten all into my stuff, I get frustrated! I like my things where they are supposed to be, in the strategic order that I placed them in. Disorder is chaotic. And chaos is ideal … said no one ever.

In the opening pages of Genesis, we find an interesting phrase that begins the creation narrative: *"Now the earth was formless and empty"* (Genesis 1:2). This is an image of disorder. But the point of the Genesis story is to help us see that God is in the business of ordering and bringing about peace through His divine intent.[3]

First, let's look at the rich meaning of the Hebrew phrase *tohu wa bohu,* translated in English as *"formless and empty"* (Genesis 1:2). *Tohu* occurs around 28 times in the Old Testament, and *bohu* is present only three times but in each instance is connected with *tohu.*[4] In Genesis 1:2, Isaiah 34:11 and Jeremiah 4:23, *bohu* relates to either chaos or emptiness. Meanwhile, *tohu* is often used in parallel with "desert" and "wilderness."[5]

Why is this important for our study of exile? Because the imagery of a wasteland contrasts strongly against the serenity and peace of home. In fact, wastelands, wildernesses and deserts are closely associated with exile in Scripture. Thematically, all these terms convey a sense of not being at home. Not at peace. In the midst of an experience that is unwanted and accompanied by pain and hardship.

And just as the earth was *tohu wa bohu* (formless, empty, wasteland), Genesis 1:2 also says *"darkness covered the surface of the watery depths."* We may think of a desert as dry and sandy, but *"watery depths"* can be a kind of wasteland too. In fact, the sea was a place of extreme fear and anxiety for people in the ancient world. The sea was unstable, could not be controlled, and was connected to ancient stories of death and destruction.

· What situations in your world today feel chaotic or empty and lead you to think, *Where is God in this?*

[3] Nahum M. Sarna, *Genesis,* The JPS Torah Commentary (Philadelphia: Jewish Publication Society, 1989), 6.
[4] William David Reyburn and Euan McG. Fry, *A Handbook on Genesis,* UBS Handbook Series (New York: United Bible Societies, 1998), 30.
[5] In Deuteronomy 32:10, for instance, *"desert" (miḏbār)* and *"wilderness" (yešimōn)* are related to *bohu.* See Victor P. Hamilton, *The Book of Genesis, Chapters 1–17,* The New International Commentary on the Old Testament (Grand Rapids, MI: William B. Eerdmans Publishing Co., 1990), 109.

· What does the Spirit of God *"hovering over the surface of the waters"* in Genesis 1:2 teach us about His presence in these situations?

We will see this pattern develop in the days and weeks ahead, but tuck this into your heart today: God's presence is always with us. He is leading us, guiding us and comforting us in the midst of the wilderness and through it. We are never left to endure alone. The presence of the Spirit in Genesis 1:2 reminds us that not even the greatest chaos or wilderness experiences of our lives can change the fact that God is in control over all things.

Ultimately, God brought chaos into order and made the watery wilderness into a world where His children could thrive. Then He *"blessed them, and God said to them, 'Be fruitful, multiply, fill the earth, and subdue it'"* (Genesis 1:28a).
· We said earlier in this study that home is the place where we can be who we are without hiding or pretense. How do you see this in Genesis 2:25? What allowed Adam and Eve to feel *"no shame"* in the home God gave them?

Where there was chaos, God established peace. And this isn't the only time we find God establishing order in the midst of watery chaos. In Mark 4:38-39, Jesus was later in a boat in the midst of a storm ... And what did He do? He brought about peace and calmed the chaos. Then in Mark 6:48-50, we find Jesus walking on water! Jesus, the One who holds all things together (Colossians 1:17) and who was with God in the very beginning (John 1:1), is in control of even the chaos.
· As we consider everything God created, bringing order and peace into the world, what does this reveal about humans since we are created in His image (Genesis 1:26-27)? How can we display God's image in our daily lives?

day 2 / GENESIS 3

Adam and Eve sinned, and all humanity was exiled as a result.

"Don't touch that!" I yelled across the store to my daughter, who saw a pretty, antique Barbie that had a huge sign over it: DO NOT TOUCH.

EmJ responded, "But, Daddy, it's so pretty. I want it!" She reached toward the doll.

Notice the pattern: She saw something beautiful and desirable. Then she determined she wanted it. And after making this determination, she reached out to take it.

Anyone hear an echo of Genesis 3? The serpent said, *"'In fact, God knows that when you eat [the forbidden fruit] your eyes will be opened and you will be like God, knowing good and evil.' The woman **saw** that the tree was good for food and delightful to look at, and that **it was desirable** for obtaining wisdom. So **she took** some of its fruit and ate it; she also gave some to her husband, who was with her, and he ate it"* (Genesis 3:5-6, emphases added).

Eve was tempted with a doubt-filled thought: *Is God actually good?*

It is important to remember here that Adam and Eve were in Eden. They were in God's royal garden, where God and humanity dwelled together. Old Testament scholar Gordon Wenham says, "Eden is not just a piece of farmland in the Mesopotamian region but an archetypal sanctuary, that is, a place where God dwells and where man should worship him."[6]

Eden was the **home** of Adam and Eve and God — and this household imagery becomes even more significant when we recall that Adam and Eve were created in the likeness and image of God (Genesis 1:26-27). The two Hebrew terms *demut ("likeness")* and *selem ("image")* in the Ancient Near Eastern context often described the unique relationship of kings or royalty and their children.[7] We can't miss this: Adam and Eve were royal children of the King of the cosmos! They lived in the household of the King, their Father.

Yet the serpent questioned Eve about the goodness of God. In the most cunning and deceptive manner, he pointed her to a source of pleasure that would ultimately lead her, Adam and all of humanity into immense pain. Genesis 3:6 shows us a pattern in the enemy's deceptions and Eve's actions (and just as culpable is Adam, who was with her).

· We mentioned this pattern in our introduction to this week, but let's review it again below, based on Genesis 3:6:

   1. She _____ that the tree was good and delightful.

   2. She reached out and _____ what she saw.

   3. She _____ and then shared with Adam.

---

[6] Gordon J. Wenham, "Sanctuary Symbolism in the Garden of Eden Story," *Proceedings of the World Congress of Jewish Studies 9* (1986), 19.

[7] In Egyptian literature, Amon Re says to Amenophis III, "Thou art my beloved son, come forth from my limbs, my very own image, which I have put upon the earth. I have permitted thee to rule over the earth in peace." This quotation makes a connection between deity, kingship and household/family in Ancient Near Eastern cultures. Cited in Claus Westermann, *Genesis 1–11*, Continental Commentary (Minneapolis: Fortress, 1994), 153-55.

- How have you seen a similar pattern in your own life? What are some ways to disrupt this pattern and resist the enemy's temptations?

- Eve invited Adam to share in her disobedience. This example shows us the power of influence we have in our relationships with others. In your relationships today, how can you use your influence in a godly way?

There are two key Hebrew words in Genesis 3:6 to pay close attention to. The first is *ra'ah*, translated into English as *"saw."* The second word is *laqah*, translated in English as *"took."* The language of *"saw"* and *"took"* is also repeated elsewhere in Scripture with the same Hebrew words, which creates a pattern to be keenly aware of.
- For instance, read the verses below, and write in your own words what each person saw and took.

  1. Genesis 12:14-15:

  2. 2 Samuel 11:2-4:

When we see things God has forbidden as beautiful and we take them for ourselves, it never ends well; we were never intended to experience those things in the first place. If we take what doesn't belong to us or let our desires lead us to destruction, the consequences are tragic. The repeated history of Scripture reinforces the importance of understanding and remembering this truth.
- For Eve and Adam, what were the consequences of their seeing and taking (Genesis 3:16-24)?

One major consequence was expulsion from Eden. They were exiled from their home. We can see the force of this in the words *"sent ... away"* and *"drove ... out"* in Genesis 3:23-24. And this physical exile of Adam and Eve was actually a representation of what already took place spiritually when they ate of the tree. Exile has both a spiritual and physical reality.

One Old Testament scholar says it this way: After the fall of humanity, "intimacy with God is replaced with alienation from God."[8] From Genesis 3 onward, all humans find themselves in exile. We have to live separated from the unique and intimate presence of God that Adam and Eve enjoyed in Eden.

But let's not forget that even in the midst of exile, there is always hope.

- Look at Genesis 3:22. Instead of allowing Adam and Eve to eat from the *"tree of life"* that would have caused them to *"live forever"* in a sinful, fallen state, how did God protect them by sending them away from the garden?

- How have you seen God working in your life or others' lives to protect you?

In Genesis 3:21, God also gave Adam and Eve animal skins to cover and protect them from the elements. And in Genesis 3:15, we have the first glimmer of the gospel, anticipating a day when the evil one would strike the promised Messiah (Jesus, an eventual *"offspring"* of Eve), but the Messiah would crush the serpent.

The rest of the story of God's people is framed by exile because sin has consequences, and the most devastating part is separation from God. But there is always hidden hope in exile. In Christ, God has a plan to bring His children back, and He gives us gifts along the way to experience His goodness. That is an encouragement and hope for us today.

---

[8] Victor P. Hamilton, *The Book of Genesis, Chapters 1–17,* The New International Commentary on the Old Testament (Grand Rapids, MI: William B. Eerdmans Publishing Co., 1990), 210.

WHO IS *Yahweh?*

Starting in Genesis 2:5, you might notice that the word *"Lᴏʀᴅ"* in your Bible is sometimes specially formatted in small caps. Why is that?

Well, in Exodus 3:13, Moses (who also wrote the book of Genesis) asked God what His name was. *"God replied to Moses, 'I AM WHO I AM'"* (v. 14a). In Hebrew, this name for God is YHWH, which is connected to the verb *hayah*, meaning "to be." It is sometimes called the "tetragrammaton" (Greek for "four-letter word") and has traditionally been translated in English Bibles as "*the Lᴏʀᴅ*" or "*I AM*."

While others who lived before Moses knew God's name very early (e.g., Seth in Genesis 4:26, Noah in Genesis 9:26, Abraham in Genesis 12:8, Isaac in Genesis 26:25, Jacob in Genesis 28:16, Laban in Genesis 30:27), God used Moses' question as a special opportunity to remind His people about His personal name and provide insight into His nature and character. "*I AM WHO I AM*" (Exodus 3:14) might sound like a circular riddle with no answer — but this actually conveys God's infinite nature!

He is self-sufficient. He is ... regardless of anything else that does or doesn't happen.
His character is immutable. He is the same yesterday, today and tomorrow.
His existence is eternal. He has always been, and will eternally be, God.
He Himself is central. God is at the center of all things.

Over time, biblical scribes began to insert vowels into the word YHWH because God's personal, covenantal name was considered too sacred to actually write down. This is where the name "Jehovah" or "Yehova" comes from. Yehova was not a spoken name for God; when reading Scripture aloud, a person would say *adonai* (meaning "sir" or "Lord") or *adoshem* (meaning "the name of the Lord"). This was so that the sacred name of God was never spoken.

In the New Testament, "Lord" (from the Greek, *kurios*, meaning "sir" or "master") is sometimes used as an equivalent for YHWH. For example, when quoting Isaiah 40:3, Jesus' disciple Matthew said, "*A voice of one crying out in the wilderness: Prepare the way for the Lord* [kurios]; *make his paths straight!*" (Matthew 3:3). But the original Old Testament passage refers to preparing the way for YHWH. Otherwise in the New Testament, "Lord" almost always refers to Jesus Christ. The Lord Jesus is the Lᴏʀᴅ God!

"*Thomas responded to [Jesus], 'My Lord and my God!'*" (John 20:28).

"*The ancestors [of Israel] are theirs, and from them, by physical descent, came the Christ, who is God over all, praised forever*" (Romans 9:5a).

day 3 / GENESIS 4:1-16

God is a God of compassion and provided protection and care even in the midst of Cain's exile.

After Adam and Eve were sent out of Eden, their family had some complicated dynamics. This is probably a relief for many of us, considering our own family dynamics!

When we read Genesis 4:1-9, we find the tragic story of the first murder in human history, and to top it off, one brother killed another out of jealousy and anger. The first question God asked Cain, the murderer, was, *"Where is your brother Abel?"* (Genesis 4:9). As we pick up in Genesis 4:10, God then asked, *"What have you done?"*

· Read Genesis 3:9 (from yesterday's study) alongside Genesis 4:9. In both verses, God spoke to Adam and Cain by asking them a question. How are these verses similar?

· God's questions led to an opportunity for repentance and restoration for both Adam and Cain — although neither of them responded rightly with a confession of their sins before God. What can we learn from this to avoid making the same error when we have sinned and separated ourselves from God?

To Cain, God said, *"Your brother's blood cries out to me from the ground"* (v. 10). The Hebrew word *sa'aq* (*"cries"*) often described the cry of those who were oppressed or afflicted.[9] This word later described the cry of people hungry for food in Genesis 41:55 and the plea of victims of injustice in Exodus 22:22-23. In the story of Cain and Abel, we find a powerful first example of how God hears the cries of His children and responds personally to them.

It's also important here to remember that Adam and Eve had been exiled from their home, Eden. They were living in the reality of exile, and so were their children. Yet in this place of exile, God still heard the cry of Abel and in response came to deal with Cain. One of the themes we will unpack throughout this week's study is the persistent presence of God, even in the midst of exile.

God's kindness, mercy, justice and righteousness coexist in ways that often surprise us. Every time we are surprised by the kindness and grace of God is a good time to celebrate and thank Him for His goodness.

[9] Victor P. Hamilton, *The Book of Genesis, Chapters 1–17,* The New International Commentary on the Old Testament (Grand Rapids, MI: William B. Eerdmans Publishing Co., 1990), 231.

- How have you experienced the kindness of God in your life recently? Write a personal example below along with a short prayer of thanks to God.

God dealt mercifully yet justly with Cain. In Genesis 4:12 we find a consequence for Cain's sin that echoed the original consequence for the sin of his father, Adam.
- Compare Genesis 3:17-19 and Genesis 4:11-12. What similarities and differences do you see?

The soil Cain worked would not cooperate with the work he put into its cultivation. Many modern commentaries suggest this implies that Cain would be exiled away from the land that had become his home.[10] Directly connected to this is the fact that Cain would be a *restless wanderer on the earth* (Genesis 4:12). The Hebrew phrase translated as *"restless wanderer"* carries the basic idea that Cain would become a "homeless wanderer." [11]

Still, God showed compassion and grace to Cain, who feared for his life as a displaced and disgraced person without any protection (Genesis 4:13-14). Even in the midst of exile, God was committed to caring for His children.

Again, there is a key pattern here: When Adam and Eve were exiled from Eden, God gave them garments of animal skin to clothe them as evidence of His care and compassion (Genesis 3:21). Now, God gave Cain a mark to protect him as evidence of His care and compassion (Genesis 4:15). Scholars debate where Cain's mark was and what it looked like, but it was immensely significant. As one scholar puts it, we should consider this mark "not [as] a stigma of infamy but [as] a sign indicating that the bearer is under divine protection."[12]

And this wouldn't be the last time God used a mark as a symbol of protection ...

[10] Gordon J. Wenham, *Genesis 1–15*, vol. 1, Word Biblical Commentary (Dallas: Word, Incorporated, 1987), 107.
[11] William David Reyburn and Euan McG. Fry, *A Handbook on Genesis*, UBS Handbook Series (New York: United Bible Societies, 1998), 116.
[12] Nahum M. Sarna, *Genesis*, The JPS Torah Commentary (Philadelphia: Jewish Publication Society, 1989), 35.

- What mark signified God's protection of the Israelites' houses in Exodus 12:13?

- According to Genesis 17:10-11, what mark did Israelite male children receive as a sign and symbol of their covenant union with God as His people?

This pattern culminates spectacularly in the New Testament: The indwelling Holy Spirit is given to all believers in Jesus as the sign and symbol of our union with God. Paul refers to this as our *"down payment"* for the inheritance we have as children of God. We are *"sealed"* with the Spirit (Ephesians 1:13-14). He is our Helper, always reminding us of God's love for us and empowering us to follow Him (John 14:26; Galatians 5:16-25).

Cain received a physical mark to protect him as he went into exile. Today, you and I are also in a type of exile in our fallen world, but we receive an invisible mark (the Spirit) that gives us protection, power and authority in Christ Jesus while we await His return.

Friend, this is our gracious God. When we are homesick and weary of wandering, God loves us, and as a very real sign and symbol of that love, He has given us a mark that is so much better than the one Cain received. We have the mark of the Holy Spirit who indwells us.

day 4 / GENESIS 6-8

God used a type of exile to save Noah and his family from the flood.

We started our study talking about how exile is the condition of being away from home. To be exiled is to be left wandering in the wilderness or to be placed in a land that is not your own. You may be able to make a home there for a time as a sojourner and stranger, but at the end of the day, it isn't the place of true belonging.

Today we are going to look at the story of Noah and see a type of exile he and his family experienced.

The story starts with the presence of ongoing sin and wickedness in the world. *"Every inclination of the human mind was nothing but evil all the time"* (Genesis 6:5), and in response to the sin that had contaminated His good creation, God would act to bring back order and peace.

· Genesis 6:8 says Noah *"found favor"* with God despite the world's brokenness. This can also be translated as "found grace." How do you think God's grace had affected Noah's life in his generation (v. 9)?

· According to Genesis 6:13-19, how would God restore order to His creation? How did He invite Noah to be a part of the restoration?

You may be hearing an echo back to Eden. The commission God gave Noah reflected the original commission God gave to Adam and Eve in Genesis 1:26: to be good stewards and caretakers of creation, specifically the animals in Eden. Instead, Adam and Eve sinned, and death entered the world. But now Noah would be God's agent of preserving the *life* of the animals, picking up where Adam and Eve failed.

· God intervened in Noah's life and used him as a means of restoration and salvation for all creation, though he was only one humble man. In what ways does this give us hope today as we ask God to use our lives for His purposes?

Genesis 7:17-24 tells us waters covered the face of the earth (creating a scene similar to Genesis 1:1) and rose so high they covered the highest mountains. All living things died except for Noah, his family, and the animals on the ark. For 150 days, they survived by floating – or we might say **wandering** – on the seas.

They were experiencing a type of exile. The only home they'd ever known was lost forever. The connection to exile is even affirmed by the prophet Isaiah, who later wrote about Israel's national exile (which we'll study in the next two weeks), "*This is like the days of Noah to me*" (Isaiah 54:9).
- How did the prophet Jeremiah similarly describe Israel's exile in Jeremiah 4:23-26?[13] How does this imagery echo Genesis 7:18-24?

The flood was devastating. Yet for Noah and his family, God intervened and provided rescue in light of Noah's righteousness (Genesis 7:1).

What we have in the story of Noah, the flood and the ark is in fact a microcosm of God's ultimate plan and vision for humanity. Yes, our exile is a response to sin and a consequence of the fall, but God is determined to have His family back together.

We will see this play out in various ways throughout Scripture, but in this specific instance, we find that the floodwaters of Genesis 6-7 were part of a divine act of *un-creation* so that the earth may be renewed, restored and ultimately *re-created* to be the ideal home for humanity. Noah, his family and the creatures with them experienced a momentary exile on the ark, but it was all for the purpose of returning to the land.
- Throughout Scripture, God demonstrates His power over water, oceans and rains, and water also symbolizes cleansing (e.g., Leviticus 16:4; Psalm 51:2). What else does God say about water in John 7:37?

- Years after God saved Noah from the flood, what kind of water now flows from those who believe in Jesus, according to John 7:38?

What a great reminder for us as we finish today's study. Exile may be our present reality, but it is not purposeless, nor is it permanent. It will not be forever for those who love and follow Jesus.

[13] Robert S. Fyall, *Now My Eyes Have Seen You: Images of Creation and Evil in the Book of Job*, ed. D. A. Carson, vol. 12, New Studies in Biblical Theology (Downers Grove, IL; England: InterVarsity Press; Apollos, 2002), 83.

The pride of humanity led to ruin and exile at Babel.

The tower of Babel is a popular Bible story to tell kids. I remember hearing this story when I was young, but rarely (if ever) did I understand the larger context of what was going on. Today we are looking at the story of Babel in Genesis 11 through a more spiritually mature lens, and to fully grasp what's taking place in Genesis 11, we need to read it within the context of Chapter 10.

In Genesis 10, we find that the families of the earth (descended from Noah after the flood we studied yesterday) had their own lands and clans with distinct languages. For example, Genesis 10:5 says *"the peoples of the coasts and islands spread out … each with its own language."*

But then in Genesis 11, *"The whole earth had the same language and vocabulary"* (Genesis 11:1). So how do you have many languages in Genesis 10 but one language in Genesis 11?

Well, Genesis 11 actually "rewinds" the historical timeline to explain how we got many languages. Humanity has always been unique and diverse in many ways, displaying God's creative handiwork, and there was both unity and diversity when one common language united all the people. However, what they *really* unified around at Babel was a rebellious action against God. They said, *"Let's build ourselves a city and a tower … Let's make a name for ourselves"* (Genesis 11:4), defying God's command to *"fill the earth"* with **His** glory (Genesis 1:28).

- How have you noticed people unifying in rebellion against God today? To be fair, many people may not think of themselves as being anti-God so much as pro-self, but this is still rebellion. Write an example or two of how this happens in our world:

Genesis 11:2 also tells us the people at Babel had *"migrated from the east."* Importantly, this was a reversal of the movement east out of Eden after Adam and Eve's exile (Genesis 3:24), followed by Cain's (Genesis 4:16). In a way, perhaps the people were attempting to reverse the exile and return home. But the problem was that they were trying to reverse an exile they had no authority to end on their own terms. God had a plan for the end of exile, as we'll begin to see in next week's study with the calling of Abraham, but at Babel, humans tried to undercut God's plan and take matters into their own hands.

Patterns have purpose, and here is a repeated pattern:

1. Adam and Eve tried to take knowledge into their own hands by eating the fruit God told them not to eat. The result? Exile.

2. Cain attempted to alleviate his anger and anxiety by killing his brother with his own hands. The result? Exile.

3. The people at Babel tried to build a tower with their own hands to make a name for themselves. The result? Exile!

Interestingly, with Noah, we actually find the pattern inverted: Noah trusted the faithful hands of God. The result? God's salvation through exile.

· What stands out to you from this biblical pattern? What are some situations in your life where you can follow Noah's example rather than the examples of Adam and Eve, Cain, or the tower builders?

It's also important that in Genesis 11:2, the people found themselves in *"a plain in the land of Shinar"* (ESV). Plains have no mountains. But people in the Ancient Near East believed God met with humanity on mountains, so in a way, they tried to build one of their own. Specifically, the tower of Babel's construction can be seen as a desire to return to Eden, *"the holy mountain of God"* (Ezekiel 28:13-14). The tower of Babel was probably a ziggurat, a type of pyramid-like "temple-tower."[14] Archaeological evidence suggests the tower of Babel was named Etemenanki, meaning "The House of the Foundation of Heaven and Earth."[15]

The desire to build this temple-tower seems to have been deeply rooted in humanity's hope to end their exile. They wanted to be reunited with God, their Father. But the way they went about it, refusing to follow God's command to *"fill the earth"* (Genesis 1:28), was an act of rebellion. The commands God gave Adam and Eve in Eden were and are still intact!

· Though the way they sought to reach Him was erroneous, God still responded to the people in Genesis 11:5-8. Where was He, and what did He do?

[14] John H. Walton notes, "We cannot say that the building project described in Genesis 11 was exclusively a temple complex, but a temple complex certainly was included and is the focus of the story." The people were likely in the beginning stages of building a large city working from the inside out. Thus, the ziggurat (step-pyramid) would have been located adjacent to the temple and near other city buildings. See John H. Walton, "The Mesopotamian Background of the Tower of Babel Account and Its Implications," *Bible and Spade* 9 (1996), 78-89.

[15] Kerr D. Macmillan, "Exegetical Theology. Review of Light on the Old Testament from Babel by Albert T. Clay," *The Princeton Theological Review* 6 (1908), 663-64.

The consequence of rebellion was the loss of the one language that provided humans with unity, understanding and common ground. This sent the people out into the world as God intended, but now they were more divided and disconnected. This was another form of exile as God's people were once again splintered due to sin.

Now, it would be easy to sit back and question or critique these people for their rebellious ways. But as a gentle reminder ... we are those people today.

How often do we try to take things into our own hands to end the exile or wilderness experience we are in the middle of? We may think if we could just do something to end it, we could get back to a place of peace and calm and feel like we are at home again. Yet even well-intentioned attempts to exalt our plans above God's lead to destruction.

- Think of a time in your life when you've rebelled against God: What were the consequences?

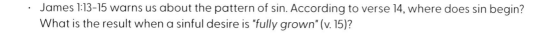

- James 1:13-15 warns us about the pattern of sin. According to verse 14, where does sin begin? What is the result when a sinful desire is *fully grown* (v. 15)?

This is such an important reminder for us to remain patient and obedient, even in the midst of our exile experience, as we wait on the Lord to bring His peace. We can trust that exile is not the end of our story; good is not just waiting for us but is actually on its way.

Even after what happened at Babel, there was amazingly good news for God's people. Next week we are going to study Abraham and find that God reached into the very heart of rebellion to enact His brilliant plan of restoration and reunion for His family.

WEEK 1 WEEKEND *Video* AND *Prayer*

As we conclude the first week of our study together, we're excited to share a special video teaching from the writer of this week's study: Dr. Joel Muddamalle, Director of Theological Research at Proverbs 31 Ministries.

Scan this QR code with your phone or visit https://first5.org/video-study to access Joel's video, where he'll share more insights about this week's scriptures and dig deeper into what we've been learning about exile.

Disclaimer: Links to additional content subject to expiration.

As you watch, feel free to jot down your notes and reflections in the space below — then join us in prayer to wrap up the week.

_____

_____

_____

_____

_____

_____

_____

_____

_____

_____

_____

_____

_____

_____

_____

_____

_____

_____

God, thank You for Your persistent presence in our lives. Even when we feel lost and far from home, help us to have eyes to see evidence of Your work and to have hearts that are attuned to You and Your desires for us. Give us the grace we need to turn from sin and turn toward You. Thank You for Your grace in the midst of exile. Help us to learn all that we can in our seasons of waiting, longing, enduring and hoping. In Jesus' name, amen.

Where is God
in our
exile?

WEEK (*Two*)

WHERE IS GOD IN OUR EXILE?

Introduction

WEEK TWO

Have you ever felt stuck in the middle? You're not at your old job anymore, but you haven't found another one. You just moved to a new town, but you haven't put down roots yet. You're between paychecks, between churches, between relationships, between seasons of life.

The middle can be scary.

The middle is full of questions.

The middle is often the place of inconsistency and instability.

The middle can feel like wilderness.

The middle is the place we are most desperate to move on from and leave behind.

But God's people often find themselves in the middle: between God's past promises and future fulfillments, between Eden and eternity. And of course, every exile experience includes a middle space between what was and what will be.

Thankfully, the middle is also a place of opportunity. It is a place of learning, longing and anticipating. It is a place of transformation. In other words, the middle always has a purpose. And smack in the middle of our own lives, we can experience profoundly the presence and power of God, who never leaves us alone. He is always with us.

So even our exile isn't without worth, and the wilderness is not void of value. But we do have to train our eyes to see the good of our exile experiences.

This week, we will look at the stories of Abraham, Jacob and Joseph, some of the most prominent figures in the history of God's people, and then we will look at Moses and the Israelites to learn from their experiences before moving on to the book of Judges. I appreciate how New Testament scholar N.T. Wright summarizes the importance of the exilic theme in these stories:

"The point of the covenant with Israel, in the whole of Scripture, is that it was the means by which God was rescuing the children of Adam and so restoring the world. And this entire narrative had to pass through the narrow door of exile, and ultimately of the cross of Jesus. This is not a side issue or a different point. It is the key to everything else."[16]

As we progress throughout the week, we will see a specific aspect of exile that directly connects to our experiences today as both a source of comfort and courage: In each of these exile moments, God's people were never left alone. They always had the presence and power of God.

[16] James M. Scott, *Exile: A Conversation with N.T. Wright* (Downers Grove, IL: IVP Academic, 2017), 75.

We might sometimes think of exile, wilderness and wandering as realities in the rearview mirror for God's people, part of the story back then in the Old Testament but not relevant for His people today. But that's not what we find in Scripture. In the weeks ahead, we will see how exile is very much relevant for us — because we're living in the middle, too, but in a different way because of the victory of Jesus on the cross. What we'll look at this week is the basis of the foundational pattern of God's presence even in His people's exile. This is a truth we can hold on to today.

— *Dr. Joel Muddamalle*

day 6 / GENESIS 12:1-3; GENESIS 16:1-12; GENESIS 21:8-19

God chose one family to be a blessing to all the nations of the world.

Last week we left off with a rebellion against God that took place at Babel. Today we're going to look at Genesis 12 and how God called one person and his family to leave the safety and security of all they'd ever known in order to follow Him and receive a new home: a promised land.

Something you may not have known is that Abram was actually living in the vicinity of Babel when God called him to *"go from [his] land"* (Genesis 12:1). Abram was first called out of *"Ur of Chaldeans"* (Genesis 11:31; Genesis 15:7), which was in Babylonia and connected to the general location of Babel (Acts 7:2-4; Joshua 24:2-3).[17] Yep, you read that right. God ended up reaching into the very epicenter of rebellion to call Abram's family out of their home and to give them a new home.

Let's take a close look at Abram's call in Genesis 12:1-3. God told Abram to exchange his current home for a land He would show him.

· Notice what God listed that Abram would have to leave: his land, his relatives and his father's home. What does this teach us about how to surrender to God as we follow Him?

· Scholars also assert that God's words to Abram in Genesis 12 were the first He had spoken to humanity in 10 generations. How does this give us hope for redemption and restoration even after a long period of what feels like silence from God?

---

[17] In Genesis 15:7, Yahweh said He brought Abraham out of *"Ur of the Chaldeans."* This designation presents the city as Babylonian (Babylonians were also called "Chaldeans"). The people there worshiped Nanna, the moon god. Within the center of the city of Ur was a fortress that held the temple of the moon god. Additionally, the ziggurat at Ur was famous. As previously noted, ziggurats were temple structures or staircases that served as entry points and a type of dwelling place for a deity. Thus, Ur served as a city center that was believed to house a deity. Essentially, Ur was a picture of a rival household of Yahweh and of rebellion against Him. See Irvin Himmel, "Abraham's Decision: To Walk by Faith (Genesis 12:1)," *Christianity Magazine* (1990), 12.

God would bless Abram, and Abram would be a blessing to the nations. On an exilic type of journey, Abram would leave his home and his family of origin, but in the end, he would become part of a greater family: God's family. And in a spectacular turn of events, through Abram, people from all nations would ultimately have the chance to be reunified into the family of God.

- Read Galatians 3:7-9. How did God ultimately use Abram to reverse the consequences of Babel, where the nations were separated and divided?

In Genesis 15:5, God promised to make Abram's family so expansive they could not be numbered. Of course, this would logically depend on Abram and his wife, Sarai, having a child. But they were unable to conceive. So in Genesis 16, Abram and Sarai (whom God later renamed Abraham and Sarah) took things into their own hands.

Remember last week what we learned about taking things into our own hands? Well, the pattern continues.

In Genesis 16, Sarah suggested that Abraham sleep with her maidservant, Hagar, so they could have a child. The result was tragic. Sarah was in pain, and she created immense pain for Hagar — and Hagar's innocent child, Ishmael. The pain and mistreatment Hagar endured was too much, and she ran away.

OK, let's pause and look at what happened next: After running away from home (essentially going into *exile*), Hagar found herself in the *wilderness*. And it was in this place, in the midst of her exile experience, that the *"angel of the LORD"* comforted her and gave her a promise that filled her with courage (Genesis 16:10-12).

- How has the Lord comforted you and reminded you of His promises in a place that felt like the wilderness? How can you join Hagar in praising God as *"the one who sees me"* (Genesis 16:13)?

This wasn't the end of Hagar's story. In Genesis 21, Abraham and Sarah finally had a child, Isaac, through God's intervention. But conflict arose between Hagar's son and Sarah's son. God told Abraham to let Hagar and her son go live someplace else because He would take care of them. So Abraham had God's assurance that things were going to be OK (Genesis 21:12-13) — but Hagar didn't!

For her, it would have been surprising when, one morning, Abraham grabbed some bread and a waterskin, gave them to Hagar, and sent her on her way.

Exile.

Hagar wandered in the wilderness of Beer-sheba until she finally ran out of water and cried as she realized this would be the end for her son (Genesis 21:14-16). At this moment, verse 17 tells us *"God heard the boy crying,"* and the angel of God spoke to Hagar once again to comfort her. When God opened her eyes, she saw a well!

· What does this show us about the goodness and provision of God for those He loves, even when they are in exile?

There are such important truths for us to grasp in today's scriptures. From Abraham, we learn exile has a purpose: God led Abraham to the promised land and blessed him to bless the nations. Exile may feel devastating and lonely at times, but we can always be aware and open to how God is working for a greater good. From Hagar, we also learn that God hears the cries of His children. He meets them in exile and journeys with them in their wilderness wandering.

· As you reflect on Abram and Hagar's experiences with the Lord, what encouragement do you find that relates to your own current situations?

12 TRIBES OF *Israel*

There are lots of characters to keep track of in the Bible! You can use this family tree as a quick reference for some important names to know as we continue learning about the origin story of Israel, God's people in the Old Testament, through the line of Abraham.

The 12 sons numbered below (in their birth order) would become the 12 tribes of Israel.

ABRAHAM + SARAH

ISAAC + REBEKAH

JACOB

+ LEAH (OLDEST SISTER)	+ ZILPAH (LEAH'S SERVANT)	+ BILHAH (RACHEL'S SERVANT)	+ RACHEL (YOUNGEST SISTER)
1 – REUBEN	7 – GAD	5 – DAN	11 – JOSEPH
2 – SIMEON	8 – ASHER	6 – NAPHTALI	12 – BENJAMIN
3 – LEVI			
4 – JUDAH			
9 – ISSACHAR			
10 – ZEBULUN			
DINAH			

day 7 / GENESIS 27; GENESIS 39:1-23

Sin led Jacob and Joseph into exile, but God's grace led them through it and back to His plan for their lives.

Today we're going to look at stories of two young men who had some significant things in common. Both upset their older brothers. Both were removed from their homes and forced into exile. Both experienced the provision of God in the midst of exile. And both were part of God's story to show us how God often uses crooked sticks to draw straight lines — in other words, He uses broken people like us to accomplish His perfect will.

Even more fascinating, these men were related: Jacob was the father, and Joseph was his son.
· The name "Jacob" in Hebrew means "supplanter," which is someone who tries to take another's place or usurp authority. How does this describe Jacob in Genesis 27?

In Genesis 27, we learn of the deceitfulness of Jacob. Influenced by his mother, Rebekah, Jacob stole the birthright of his older brother, Esau.

Needless to say, Esau was furious, and he said he would murder Jacob. (Hear an echo of an elder brother desiring to murder the younger brother? Look back at Cain and Abel in Genesis 4.) Rebekah, hearing of Esau's plan, sent Jacob to live with her brother Laban in Haran (Genesis 27:43-45). So Jacob was sent away from home — exiled — to live in a land not his own, all because of his selfishness and sin.
· But God's plan for Jacob's future remained. Read Genesis 28:13-15, and list what God said He would do for and through Jacob. How did Jacob respond in verses 16-17?

· Consider some times in your own life, even when you felt far from home, when God reminded you of His promises and humbled you to say, *"Surely the LORD is in this place, and I did not know it"* (Genesis 28:16).

Jacob eventually returned home after he was deceived by his uncle Laban and found himself married to two women: Leah and Rachel. He ended up having eight sons with Leah and her servant Zilpah and four sons with Rachel and her servant Bilhah; these would become the 12 tribes of Israel, God's people in the Old Testament.

One of Jacob's sons was Joseph. And let's just say ... the apple didn't fall far from the tree. Joseph, like his father, created a whole mess with his brothers. Some interpretations of Genesis 37 suggest young Joseph was arrogant, prideful and seriously lacked self-awareness.

- How do you see these characteristics of Joseph in Genesis 37:3-11?

Eventually Joseph was captured by his own brothers, who threw him into a pit to sell him into slavery in Egypt. Once again, we find the younger brother in exile (forcibly removed from his home).

But there is also this interesting detail in Genesis 39:2: *"The LORD was with Joseph, and he became a successful man, serving in the household of his Egyptian master."*

Why is this important? A few reasons. First, in Joseph's exile, God was with him. And this reality is directly connected to the success Joseph experienced in the household of his master, Potiphar. Second, it's important to remember the humanity of the text here: Joseph was likely so grateful for the success and opportunity God gave him, but we can imagine he went to bed at night longing for his own home. Wishing things were different.

Tonight you may have the very same complicated feelings. Things seem to be going well in some areas, and you are so thankful to God for that. But other things aren't what you wished. And that sorrow has to live somehow in the midst of gratitude.

This is what Joseph may have felt when his roller-coaster journey took even more sharp turns:

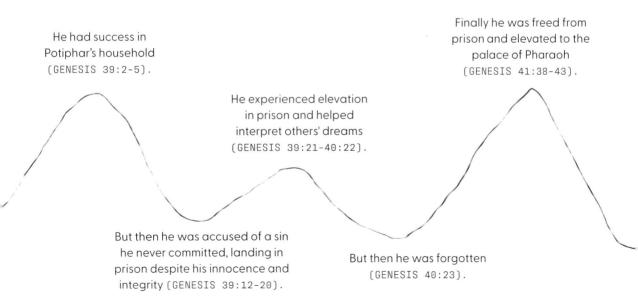

He had success in Potiphar's household (GENESIS 39:2-5).

Finally he was freed from prison and elevated to the palace of Pharaoh (GENESIS 41:38-43).

He experienced elevation in prison and helped interpret others' dreams (GENESIS 39:21-40:22).

But then he was accused of a sin he never committed, landing in prison despite his innocence and integrity (GENESIS 39:12-20).

But then he was forgotten (GENESIS 40:23).

- As you think about your own life, list a few highs and lows. How does your journey reflect that the Lord has been with you through it all, just as He was with Joseph?

Genesis 39:21 says, "*The Lord was with Joseph and extended kindness to him. He granted him favor.*" In Joseph's exile, God was present. It was God who made him successful. It was also God who showed him kindness. And this is also true for us.

Both Jacob and Joseph experienced exile, sadness, hardship, and things they never wanted to endure. But in the midst of it all, our good God was present with them. In the end, they both were reunited with their family and experienced God's goodness in their exile seasons.

We may be facing some very difficult things we wish weren't so. And it is completely OK to have feelings of sadness, loneliness and angst. But let's make the decision today that when we feel those emotions, we also respond with the truth: *Yes, I'm feeling this. And yes, God is with me in it. I am not alone.*
- What might look different in your life today if you responded to your emotions with this perspective?

God is committed to His family, and He will be present with us in the midst of hard things, which makes them some of the most holy things. That's exactly the story of Israel — which we will continue studying tomorrow.

day 8 / EXODUS 1:1-14; EXODUS 3:7-10

Even in their exile, God saw, heard and knew about His people's affliction and acted to bring about their rescue.

At the end of Joseph's story, which we read yesterday, God used Joseph to save many lives (Genesis 50:20). This included the lives of his brothers and his father, Jacob; they left Canaan (the promised land given to Abraham) during a famine and joined Joseph in Egypt as a place of shelter and refuge. In Egypt, Joseph's family — who became known as the Israelites — multiplied despite living in a land that was not their own.

Exodus 1:7 says it this way: *"The Israelites were fruitful, increased rapidly, multiplied, and became extremely numerous so that the land was filled with them."* But after Joseph and his immediate family died, a new Egyptian Pharaoh rose to power, and he panicked at the sheer strength and number of the Israelites (Exodus 1:8-10). Soon they were enslaved.

It's important to note here that Egypt wasn't originally a place of exile. It was actually a place God assigned for the Israelites as a refuge (Genesis 50:20-22) — but over time, the place of refuge became the very place they were exiled and imprisoned.

· Can you think of a situation in your own life that started out well but, over time, and ended in suffering or started to feel like a prison? What got you through? What lessons did you take with you from that season?

· Look up Genesis 15:13-16. What had God previously told Abraham about the future of his descendants, and how was this fulfilled through the Israelites' exile in Egypt?

Even with the prophecy from Genesis 15, there are some things we don't know: Did God warn the Israelites to leave Egypt before Pharaoh enslaved them? How were they supposed to know when to leave? One thing we do know is that Joseph indicated the Israelites were not supposed to stay in Egypt permanently. Before he died, he pleaded with his family to take his bones back home to Canaan:

"Joseph said to his brothers, 'I am about to die, but God will certainly come to your aid and bring you up from this land to the land he swore to give to Abraham, Isaac, and Jacob … When God comes to your aid, you are to carry my bones up from here'" (Genesis 50:24-25).

Sometimes we find ourselves in a season similar to the Israelites in Egypt: At first, everything seems good. Our lives are fruitful. There seems to be momentum. Then ... things shift. The good things are exchanged for hard ones. What was once fruitful is now barren. The momentum screeches to a stop, and it may even feel like we are in reverse. It's hard to process that our location hasn't changed, but everything else has.

- In these moments, how can we remember that, as Joseph said in Genesis 50:24, "*God will certainly come to [our] aid*"?

What Joseph said on his deathbed did come true for Israel. God did bring them out of their exile and into the land of promise. Let's take a close look at Exodus 3:7-10 to see how.

God used the first-person pronoun "I" nine times in these four verses. This language invites us to reflect on how personal God is. In verses 7-8 (emphases added below), He said:

- *"**I have observed** the misery of my people ..."*
- *"**I know** about their sufferings ..."*
- *"**I have come down** to rescue them ..."*

"*I have come down*" might make us think we're about to see Jesus walking the earth — God in human form! But that didn't happen until later. Instead, for now, in a surprising turn of events, God sent a man named Moses to lead the Israelites out of their exile and captivity in Egypt and eventually into the promised land God had for them (Exodus 3:10).

- Genesis 11:5 tells us God *"came down"* to scatter sinful people into exile at Babel, yet Exodus 3:8 says He would also *"come down to rescue"* His people from exile. What does this reveal about the nature and character of God?

- According to Exodus 3:8, what would the land be like that God promised to Israel? How was this different from what they experienced under the oppression of Egypt?

What God said in Exodus 3:7-10 is still true today. Whatever situation you find yourself in, you can be assured that God observes, hears and knows everything, and He is acting to rescue and restore you.

If you have any doubt about that, look to Jesus. The Israelites had Moses as their leader, but we have the greater Moses: Christ. We're going to talk about this in detail in Week 4 of our study, but for now, we can begin to consider how Jesus has *come down to rescue* us (Exodus 3:7) and bring an end to exile for all who trust in Him. The spiritual exile that began in Eden ended on the cross. And someday Jesus will come again to bring us home forever.

To end our time today, let's rest in this truth: God sees, hears and knows, and not only has He acted but He is continually acting on our behalf.

day 9 / # NUMBERS 13-14

Because God's people disobeyed Him, they were sent to wander in the wilderness for 40 years.

We all know how it feels to think, *It shouldn't have gone this way.* I bet the Israelites felt the same way a few years into their wilderness wandering.

The story should have gone like this: The Israelites trusted God because of His past faithfulness, knowing He would continue to be faithful to them in their present situation. God had miraculously delivered them out of Egypt (Exodus 7-14) and now told them to take the promised land of Canaan, which had become inhabited by pagan peoples while the Israelites were in Egypt for 400 years. The Isralites should have recalled the long history of God's faithfulness and obeyed what He said.

But ... that's not how the story went. Instead, Israelite spies went into Canaan, and the majority of them were terrified by the size and strength of the inhabitants. Because of fear, they gave a negative report to the rest of the Israelites in Numbers 13:31-33.
- But let's not miss Numbers 13:30 and Numbers 14:6-8. Who spoke up with positive words about the task ahead? Why were they so confident?

God had done amazing miracles for the Israelites as He led them out of Egypt: He guided them in a pillar of fire by night and in a pillar of cloud by day (Exodus 13:21). He parted the Red Sea to allow them to walk through (Exodus 14). The Israelites could have remembered all these experiences – but instead, they complained. They believed Moses and his brother Aaron, led by God, had brought them out of Egypt only so they could die in the wilderness (Numbers 14:1-2). They lost sight of their home, the promised land, because of fear.
- Identify a situation when you faced fear about doing something God had told you to do. What was the cost of your disobedience or the reward for your obedience? Reflect on the lessons you learned.

Fear robs us of our clarity. It suggests we are less than we actually are or tempts us to try to be more than we are in order to overcome the fear. Both of these responses are not only unhelpful but actually sinful, distrusting of God. Fear in and of itself isn't necessarily bad, but what we do in response to fear is of utmost importance.

The Israelites responded to fear by rejecting and doubting God. The consequence was severe: God said, *"None of those who have despised me will see [the promised land]"* (Numbers 14:23b). Instead, they would experience — you guessed it — exile. Specifically, 40 years of wandering in the wilderness.

First, God actually said He would destroy all the Israelites as just punishment for their unbelief (Numbers 14:12), but Moses pleaded with God to show mercy. Moses recalled how God had been with His people through every step of their journey (Numbers 14:13-16). If God destroyed the Israelites now, the nations might think *"the Lord wasn't able to bring this people into the land he swore to give them"* (Numbers 14:16).

Can someone say, "Thank goodness for Moses!"? God responded in Numbers 14:20 by sparing the Israelites from immediate death, but He still gave them a consequence for their sin. Once again, we see a pattern: God gave His children kindness and compassion they didn't deserve, even as they went into exile. In other words: grace. Here we find a retelling of the Eden story, where God gave Adam and Eve grace even as they were banished from the garden (Genesis 3:21-22).

- Grace means "unmerited favor." While our sinful decisions have undesirable consequences, we serve a God who leads us back to Him. What does Romans 2:4 say about God's kindness?

- Think of a time when you deserved judgment but received mercy. In response, write a prayer of praise and gratitude to God:

God also showed grace to Caleb and Joshua, whom He allowed to enter the promised land because of their loyalty to Him. Here we find a retelling of Abraham's story (and Noah's too!), in which God reached into the epicenter of rebellion and chose to save a faithful few.

- What do the examples of Caleb and Joshua, Noah, and Abraham reveal about God's response to individual obedience in the midst of corporate disobedience?

- Where is the Lord calling you to obey Him even when those around you are not?

Friend, obedience in the midst of our wilderness is worth it. God sees it and rewards it.
And in a further surprising spin, rather than fulfilling the greatest fear of the Israelites — that their children would be plundered (Numbers 14:3) — God said He would do the very opposite. "*I will bring your children whom you said would become plunder into the land you rejected, and they will enjoy it*" (Numbers 14:31).

It's easy to overlook these details, but notice how personal verse 31 is: "*I will bring …*" Though the children would live out a wilderness experience due to their parents' distrust of God, He would be with them and deliver them from the wilderness to bring them home to the promised land.

As we end today, here are two things we can reflect on: First, our obedience in the middle of exile matters. Second, God has always been faithful and present to lead His people personally through the wilderness to the promises He has in store.

day 10 / JUDGES 2:11-15; JUDGES 17:6

When Israel rejected and neglected God as King, the consequence was self-imposed exile.

As we've studied Scripture, we've seen how exile is the opposite of the safety, security and belonging of being at home. Some of us may have an idealized view of "home" from watching TV shows like The *Brady Bunch, Family Matters* or *Full House*. The first few minutes of each show start with everything going awesomely — then something goes wrong, only to be nicely and neatly resolved with peace and harmony in 30 minutes flat. Who wouldn't want that?

But often it isn't that simple. Family can be complicated — so much so that maybe you don't have positive memories or experiences of home. Still, God created us all with a longing to belong, not in a sitcom setting but in a *true home* filled with the love of God Himself. Because what really makes a safe and secure home is the presence of love inside it. In this way, home is so much more than a place. It involves the people who take up residence in that place.

- How would you describe the ideal home? More than what it would look like, what would it feel like, provide or mean to you?

In the book of Judges, the Israelites had finally gotten to the promised land. However, they didn't do what God asked them to do to make this land their home: drive out the pagan nations that inhabited it and the idol worship that came with them.

- Based on Judges 2:11-15, how would you summarize what happened when Israel did not honor and love God as the head of their home?

I don't know about you, but what I want in a place I call "home" is peace. And none of this sounds peaceful: constant attacks from enemies, raids from marauders, enslavement, turmoil, disaster, suffering ...

So what happened? The people lost their focus on God.

- What word is repeated in Judges 2:11-15 to describe God's feelings toward Israel because of their disobedience (failing to drive out their enemies from the land)?

- Though God was angry with Israel and allowed their suffering, what does Judges 2:16-18 show about His care for them?

Here's the thing: It's not like we just lose focus on God and that's the end of it. We actually end up in an *exchange* of focus. For the Israelites, they exchanged their focus, attention and affection from God to false gods.[18] By going after these false gods, they rejected the true God. They gave up their sure and certain source of safety and security for a counterfeit source.
- While today it's less common for people to set up statues to worship as idols, what "counterfeits" might capture our hearts and imaginations? (Keep in mind that an idol can be anything we value or love more than God: money, achievement, family, etc.)

Old Testament scholars refer to a "cycle of sin" in Judges:

1. Israel turned away from God and did evil.
2. God saw the evil acts of His people and responded in justice by executing His judgment.
3. Israel cried out or wept to the Lord.
4. God heard the cries and delivered the Israelites through various judges, or rescuers He chose and equipped to help His people.

Then, eventually, they turned away from God again, and the cycle continued.

One truth this reveals is that Canaan was a good and beautiful land; however, the presence and favor of God Himself was what made it a **homeland**. By rebelling against God, the people forfeited the belonging, joy and peace that could have been theirs.

In Judges 17:6, we see that *"in those days there was no king in Israel; everyone did whatever seemed right to him."* Now, what does this actually mean? Does this suggest that Israel needed a king? Or is this an indictment against Israel for rejecting God as their King?

[18] Joel Muddamalle, *Finding Peace Through Humility: A Bible Study in the Book of Judges* (Harper Christian Resources, 2024).

It's both. God was their King (their government was a "theocracy"), which takes us back to the garden of Eden. God is a good King and Father to His children. What happens when those children reject Him? Things turn chaotic.

- As you reflect on the cycle of sin in Judges, what steps might the Lord be leading you to take to walk away from chaotic counterfeits and toward Him?

This is an important lesson for us as we finish our study this week. It's possible to be at home but not have the comfort, safety and security that come from a loving family or head of household. This means we can be at home physically and still go through a type of wilderness experience spiritually, like the Israelites when they lived in the promised land but rejected the God of the promises.

Yet the reverse is also true: We can be in physical exile and still feel the spiritual benefits and safety of home — if we embrace the Father who is with us on our journey. God our Father offers kindness and protection when we live under His loving authority and seek His presence.

Even when the Israelites were exiled in Egypt, then in the wilderness, and finally during the time of judges, there was a purpose to all of this. God was encouraging His family to be persistent in obedience and faithfulness in the midst of exile and then watch and see how He would bring the beauty and comfort of home to them.

Friend, if you feel like you are in a cycle that's spiraling out of control, there is a way out. It starts with embracing God, which leads to obedient and faithful living, then waiting and watching as God brings safety, security and strength.

WEEK 2 WEEKEND *Video* AND *Prayer*

As we conclude Week 2 of our study together, we're excited to share another video teaching from the writer of this week's study, Dr. Joel Muddamalle.

Scan the QR code or visit https://first5.org/video-study to access Joel's video, where he'll share more insights about this week's scriptures and dig deeper into what we've been learning about exile.

*Disclaimer: Links to additional content subject to expiration.

As you watch, feel free to jot down your notes and reflections in the space below — then join us in prayer to wrap up the week.

God, thank You for reminding us that our obedience in the midst of exile matters. You are our King and our loving Father, and You desire to lead Your people for our ultimate good and for Your total glory. Help us become aware of the temptations that are presented to us, and give us strength not to put our trust in anything else but You. In Jesus' name, amen.

who can
end
our exile?

WEEK (*Three*)

WHO CAN END OUR EXILE?

Introduction

WEEK THREE

Suffering and separation can be so discouraging. The loneliness and discomfort of exile leave us longing for change – for a day when relationships aren't complicated, jobs aren't lost, and sickness doesn't lead to death. But this week, God's Word will remind us that exile doesn't last forever for God's people and that we have lessons to learn even in the midst of our wilderness experiences.

The exiles we'll read about this week weren't just for nations but also for individuals, from kings to prophets, everyday people, families, tribes and communities. We'll find that individual exile has communal impacts, and communal exile also works its way back to the individual. But most importantly, as we study examples like King David running from Saul in the wilderness, and the prophet Elijah fleeing from Queen Jezebel, we will come to recognize that when we aren't sure where we belong on earth, we can always run toward the Lord. He won't shame us when we feel beaten down by a world wracked with sin. The Lord gave David favor while he was living as a nomad, and He fed and comforted Elijah with rest.

We may not always feel settled and secure on this planet, but we can hold

on to the truths that exile is temporary for God's people and that we belong with our Creator. As believers, we will be with Jesus forever – and forever actually starts right now! One day, Jesus will return to bring us to our eternal home, but He is also with us today, and His Spirit dwells within us. Until Jesus returns to this earth or we depart from it in death and go to Him, we can stand on His promises and learn to obey His words in Scripture.

The nation of Israel, as we will see, brought exile upon themselves by failing to listen to God. They watched their relatives drift from the Lord and fall into idolatry, but they didn't respond when prophets like Jeremiah called them to repent from their sins. Eventually, God's people were carried into captivity by nations like Babylon and Assyria that did not fear Him.

However, even this was part of God's redemptive plan. From the Israelites' mistakes, we learn to stay close to the Lord and not heap suffering upon ourselves through disobedience. Yet we also learn that the Lord can and will use anything in His creation – even exile in seemingly godless places – to bring about His ultimate good.

As we study together, let's look back at the past and learn, but let's also look forward with hope to the day when we will no longer struggle against the world, the flesh and the devil. Each of the exiles we'll look at this week had an endpoint ordained by God – which reminds us in our own wilderness seasons that things will not always be the way they are now. And while we wait for Christ's return to end our exile forever, we can feast on God's Word, which encourages us.

We'll end this week by talking about a period of 400 years when God seemed silent – but today we know God is always speaking through His Holy Spirit and His Word. We don't want to live in a self-imposed exile from hearing God's voice because we let our Bibles gather dust. So let's open up the Scriptures and dive in together!

— *Melissa Spoelstra*

day 11 / 1 SAMUEL 22:1-2; 1 KINGS 12

Israel and Judah divided into two separate kingdoms.

We wrapped up last week talking about how God provided judges to help His people when they had no king. This week, we'll talk about a later era in Israel's history when they did have kings ... but these human rulers didn't solve all their problems. In fact, studying Israel's kings increases our longing for God's Kingdom more than any earthly home.

At some times during the period of the kings in biblical history, the people of God experienced a sense of national identity and belonging. Nonetheless, from the very beginning, the kings were imperfect leaders: Israel's first king, Saul, ultimately rebelled against the Lord (1 Samuel 15:22-23). Then when God chose David to become Israel's new king, Saul tried to kill him, driving David into the wilderness.

- · Read 1 Samuel 22:1-2, and describe the people who fled to live in caves along with David when he was fleeing Saul. How did the people feel at this time?

David spent 13 years running from Saul. He moved from place to place along with others who had their own stories of individual exile.

But during this difficult season in David's life, God showed grace and favor in the midst of his brokenness. For example, when *"Saul and his men were closing in on David and his men to capture them,"* God enabled David to escape (1 Samuel 23:26-28).

- · When you've experienced a dark season, feeling disillusioned and lacking a sense of belonging, how have you seen God provide for you and protect you?

Eventually David did become king as God promised, and the reigns of David and his son Solomon ushered in a season of prosperity in Israel, including victories in battle, material wealth and status for the nation. Solomon also built a temple for God in Israel. The temple was the place where heaven met earth: Scholar N.T. Wright says, "When you went up to the temple, it was not *as though* you were 'in heaven.' You were *actually* there" (emphases added). As foreign as it may be to our modern worldview, for the ancient Jew, "heaven and earth were always made to work together, to interlock and overlap."[19] God's people brought sacrifices, offered prayers, sought wisdom and looked for deliverance at the temple because God's presence was there.

---

[19] James M. Scott and N.T. Wright, *Exile: A Conversation with N. T. Wright* (Westmont, IL: InterVarsity Press, 2017), 37-38.

The concepts of kingship and the temple were closely tied together in Israel. However, the kingdom itself eventually became broken and divided: King Solomon's son Rehoboam couldn't hold the tribes together, and 10 northern tribes separated as the nation of Israel while two southern tribes formed the nation of Judah. In this divided kingdom, a sense of national and spiritual exile rippled throughout the land once again.

· Based on 1 Kings 12, draw a line to match the people on the left with their descriptions on the right to review how Israel's kingdom became divided:

REHOBOAM — Rehoboam's taskmaster, who was stoned to death by the Israelites when he came to collect taxes after they seceded (v. 18).

JEROBOAM — Solomon's son (v. 6), who followed the advice of bad advisors and gave a harsh reply to the leaders of the 10 northern tribes (vv. 13-14).

ADORAM — The man of God who warned Rehoboam not to fight against the rebellious tribes because the kingdom's fracture was actually *"from"* the Lord (vv. 22-24).

SHEMAIAH — The man who led a revolt against Rehoboam's rule and became king of the northern tribes of Israel. He said going to the temple to worship God was *"too difficult"* and encouraged idol worship (v. 28).

· In 1 Kings 12:16, God's people said they had lost their *"portion"* or *"inheritance"* in the divided kingdom. Read Numbers 34:1-2 for a quick reminder about what inheritance meant to the Israelites. How does losing an inheritance relate to exile?

Reading these scriptures can feel discouraging. But just when we wonder how there could be any hope left for God's people ... 1 Kings 12:15 notes that God was sovereignly guiding His people even through their brokenness: *"This turn of events came from the Lord to carry out his word, which the Lord had spoken."*

This may not sit well with us when we consider how the Lord might be allowing our own seasons of brokenness. But when we remember that much of the Bible is about people who experienced long seasons of exile — from royalty to regular people just like you and me — we can take heart. When we are tempted to wonder if this life is as good as it gets, we can hold on to hope, knowing this world in its current state of brokenness is not meant to meet our longing for belonging. Our hope is not in an earthly king, temple or kingdom. Instead, we set our sights on Jesus, the true King who will set all things right.

- As you consider David's personal exile and the corporate exile of the northern tribes from Judah and Benjamin, what stands out most to you? Where do you catch glimpses of God's purposes through these exiles?

day 12 / 1 KINGS 19:1-8

Elijah rested after he encountered rejection.

After God's people divided into the northern tribes of Israel and the southern tribes of Judah, the fractured nation continued to experience increasing chaos because of increasing sin. Idolatry and rebellion characterized the nation of Israel in the north, though the people had once followed Yahweh. Yet God in His mercy sent prophets to call His people to turn from their sin and turn back to Him.

Today we'll read about Elijah, who was one of these prophets. He decreed three years without rain as God's judgment on His rebellious people (1 Kings 17:1). At the time, the evil King Ahab and his wife, Jezebel, ruled the land and promoted the worship of Baal – a pagan god of rain – so God's ability to withhold rain proved His supremacy as the Almighty. Elijah's drought also ended with a contest between Yahweh and Baal on Mount Carmel, which God won, providing more supernatural proof of His power (1 Kings 18:20-41).

After this, Elijah may have envisioned a new era of godliness and commitment to God's commands in Israel. Maybe the people would repent and return to God, and Israel would start to feel like "home" again!
- But according to 1 Kings 19:1-4, summarize in your own words what actually happened. (Note: *"The prophets"* in verse 1 were the false prophets of Baal who were defeated on Mount Carmel.)

King Ahab had watched God demonstrate His power firsthand, but he didn't change his ways. Instead, he seemed to fear Jezebel more than the one true God. This reminds us that having faith means more than just seeing evidence of who God is. One commentator points out, "Sometimes Christians slip into thinking that if we only get the truth to people or press upon them our most rigorous and cogent arguments, then [they will love God]... But let Jezebel be your teacher about what the human heart is like. There was a blaze of light on Mt. Carmel, but unless Yahweh grants internal light to see his external light, darkness remains."[20]

This darkness that still held God's people captive moved Elijah to despair. First Kings 19:3 says Elijah *"ran for his life,"* going into exile in the wilderness, because he *"became afraid,"* which is translated from a Hebrew verb that could also mean "to see how things are."[21]

We can likely relate to Elijah when we see things as they are in our lives. Maybe we thought a trial was ending, but instead we find more problems to face and more battles to fight. When it comes to parenting, marriage, health issues, work and ministry situations, we may want to run away at times. We may not be running from death but from the constant challenges of life.

[20] Dale Ralph Davis, *1 Kings: The Wisdom and The Folly, Focus on the Bible Commentary Series*, (Ross-shire, Scotland: Christian Focus Publications, 2002), 267.
[21] Iain W. Provan, *Understanding the Bible Commentary Series: 1 & 2 Kings*, (Grand Rapids, IL: Baker Books, 1995), 138.

- What are some situations where you might feel like saying, *"I have had enough!"* like Elijah did in verse 4, and how can you ask God to bring hope to those situations?

Elijah was in such despair he prayed for death in verse 4 – but God had a different ending for his exile, and while we might relate to his despair, we know there are better prayers to be prayed. Still, God didn't shame Elijah for human emotions on the other side of a holy exertion.
- Read 1 Kings 19:4-9, and describe God's care for Elijah in these moments:

When we are tired and hungry, especially in a season that feels like exile, our fears and doubts can multiply. So God ensured that Elijah slept, ate and drank. Then he slept some more and ate and drank again (vv. 5-8). We, too, need time for soul care and physical rest to prepare us for journeys ahead.
- List some specific examples of how physical hunger and fatigue can affect you spiritually. How might caring for your physical needs be a part of how you care for your soul?

Elijah needed both physical and spiritual strength to travel to Mount Sinai, where God filled him with a new sense of purpose and led him out of exile – out of the wilderness (1 Kings 19:8-21). Whether our travels are geographical or mental and emotional, we also need times of rest. When we have been running hard through spiritual highs and lows, we often need a broom tree like the one Elijah slept under (v. 5).
- What are some practical ways the Lord might be calling you to prioritize rest in the coming week?

day 13 / # 2 KINGS 17:1-23

Assyria conquered and exiled Israel.

Much of our suffering on earth is a side effect of living on a planet under the curse of sin. When terrible and tragic things happen, we don't always know why — often there is no specific explanation other than the fact that our world is a broken place.

However, in some cases, we can recognize painful consequences in our lives that result from our own bad choices. Thankfully, God can use even those consequences for redemptive purposes.

This is what happened when Israel continued in their idolatry despite the warnings of prophets like Elijah. Today we'll read about the fall of the northern tribes in Israel as they were exiled to Assyria — but it's important to remember that leading up to this exile, the Lord had clearly expressed His expectations for His people. He also sent warnings through many prophets: Elijah, Elisha, Amos and Hosea were among those God raised up to preach a message of repentance that was not heeded (2 Kings 17:13-14).

Here we find echoes of another exile: In the garden of Eden, God clearly warned Adam and Eve not to eat from the tree of the knowledge of good and evil (Genesis 2:17), and their disobedience resulted in exile. In the same way, God forewarned His people in Israel that their disobedient decisions would have consequences. We even see this forewarning when God delivered His people from Egypt and reminded them of His instructions for living in the promised land.

· Read Deuteronomy 30:15-20. How would you summarize in your own words the postures that God said would lead to blessings (vv. 16, 20)?

· What behaviors and heart attitudes would bring exile for God's people (vv. 17-18)?

· What did the Lord want them to choose (v. 19)?

Now let's fast-forward to 200 years after Solomon's glorious rule of Israel. The northern tribes no longer worshipped in Jerusalem as the Lord prescribed. Instead, as we read a few days ago, King Jeroboam set up golden calves – one on each end of the kingdom – so the people could worship them in a false religion (1 Kings 12:26-30). The kings who succeeded Jeroboam continued to perpetuate evil practices.

- To learn what eventually happened, review 2 Kings 17:1-23, and note any references to God's warnings:

From the time they came into the promised land, the Lord warned His people not to worship idols (2 Kings 17:12). God had driven out the nations that practiced idolatry, divination (fortune-telling via false gods), and human sacrifice, but instead of rejecting these behaviors, Israel copied them. Now God's people would suffer an exile much like the Canaanites they emulated. Both groups were driven from their homeland, *"dispossessed"* (v. 8) and *"banished … from his presence"* (v. 20).

So Israel went into exile in Assyria. And it seems that for these northern tribes, restoration has not yet occurred: No historical record exists of these people returning to their land. Hence, they are sometimes referred to as the "lost tribes" of Israel.

In Ezekiel, Scripture speaks of a future restoration of the 12 tribes and therefore an end to exile (Ezekiel 37:15-22). N.T. Wright suggests this prophecy points to Jesus and the calling of His 12 disciples (one for every tribe). In that sense, the exile has already ended for Israel. The Messiah has come. But in another sense, since the consummation of God's Kingdom will not be fully realized until Jesus' return, some point out this was only the beginning of the end of exile, and both Jews and non-Jews who have turned to Jesus as King are still in a sort of exile today.[22]

We stand alongside the lost tribes, waiting for God to rescue us from life on a fallen planet. Yet in the meantime, we can also consider God's warnings and how He calls us away from idolatry and toward Himself today. We may not be wearing an "I love Baal" T-shirt or setting up Asherah poles in our yards, but we still struggle with counterfeit gods. Tim Keller defines idolatry as "anything more important to you than God. Anything that absorbs your heart and imagination more than God. Anything you seek to give you what only God can give."[23]

[22] James M. Scott, Exile: *A Conversation with N.T. Wright,* (Downers Grove, IL: IVP Academic, 2017), 204.
[23] Timothy Keller, *Counterfeit Gods: The Empty Promises of Money, Sex, and Power, and the Only Hope that Matters* (New York, NY: Penguin, 2009), xvii.

A NOTE ON *Idols:*

Sometimes idols are sneaky. They may not be things that we consider **more** important than God, but without knowing it, we put them on a level with God. Idols may be things we really like: our jobs, our friends, our kids, our pets, our lifestyle, etc. But God deserves our highest attention, love and honor. He belongs in a completely separate category above everything and everybody. In addition, idols may even be placed below God in our hearts but keep us from loving our neighbor. Does our love for our pets, for example, come before loving the people God has placed in our life? Let's love God and people, not idols!

· What potential idols in your life come to your mind as you think about the above definition? How can you turn your heart and imagination to God alone?

We want to learn from the Israelites to heed God's warnings and be faithful to Him. Today's reading reminds us we can experience spiritual exile when we allow anything to take God's place in our hearts ... but as long as we draw breath, our loving Father continually calls us back to Himself. Second Kings 17:39 reminds us of this promise: *"Fear the LORD your God, and he will rescue you from all your enemies."*

day 14 / 2 KINGS 25:1-21

Babylon conquered and exiled Judah.

After Assyria exiled the northern tribes of Israel in 722 B.C., which we read about yesterday, the southern kingdom of Judah escaped Assyrian threats because the Lord delivered them. The prophet Isaiah encouraged King Hezekiah of Judah to trust the Lord, and God supernaturally delivered Judah from Assyrian threats of war (2 Kings 18:13-19:37).

Unfortunately, after this deliverance, Judah did not stay the course of trusting Yahweh. Over time, they drifted into some of the same sins that had hastened Israel's exile.
- What specific reasons for Israel's exile did we discover in yesterday's study? (Hint: See 2 Kings 17:15.) What are some ways we can avoid spiritually drifting away from the God who is our Deliverer?

Over 100 years later, Judah had witnessed Israel's exile but apparently had not learned from it. Still, God continued to send His prophets with warnings to motivate the people to return to Him.

- One such prophet was Jeremiah. Finish each sentence from Jeremiah 18:6-11 in your own words to record God's promises and exhortations:

    · Like clay is in the potter's hand, so is _____ (v. 6).

    · If a nation turns from its evil ways, God will _____ (v. 8).

    · _____ now from your evil ways, and correct your ways and your deeds (v. 11).

- As you consider God's message to Judah in Jeremiah 18:6-11, what encouragement or conviction resonates in your life today?

Jeremiah wasn't the only one encouraging the nation of Judah to repent. The prophet Isaiah had written words of warning 100 years prior. Ezekiel, Daniel, Joel, Micah, Zephaniah and Habakkuk also called the people to remember the past and consider the future.

But their disobedience continued. And 2 Kings 25 tells us the result: *"Judah went into exile from its land"* (v. 21b).

- Based on 2 Kings 25:1-2, how many years was the city of Jerusalem under siege?

- How were "*the house of the LORD,*" the houses of the people, and the walls of the city impacted by Babylon's invasion (vv. 9-10, 13-17)? What was the fate of the people and priests (vv. 11-12, 18-21)?

This account of Judah's exile is heartbreaking. But we can remember Judah's story wasn't finished; later, through the decree of King Cyrus of Persia, God allowed many exiles to come back to their land. And through their 70 years of suffering in Babylon, God helped them answer the question, *Where and what is our true home?* Returning to their promised land itself didn't solve all their issues of identity and belonging, but they returned with a greater understanding of their dependence on their Maker.

This generation of oppression also shaped the way Israel's story was shared with future descendants. As the surviving exiles passed down their oral history, their stories would have been framed within the context of their own experiences of war, relocation and displacement. They wept at times when they compared their land with its past glory. Yet this actually served as a reminder that for God's people to truly be at home, they needed more than a restored place on earth — they needed a restored relationship with God.

And God told them of a day when full restoration would come. The prophet Isaiah recorded this promise from God in the final verses of his book:

"For I will create new heavens and a new earth; the past events will not be remembered or come to mind. Then be glad and rejoice forever in what I am creating; for I will create Jerusalem to be a joy and its people to be a delight" (Isaiah 65:17-18).

Isaiah went on to describe a time when there will be no tears and no death, but instead there will be beautiful homes and bountiful produce: *"People will build houses and live in them; they will plant vineyards and eat their fruit. They will not build and others live in them; they will not plant and others eat"* (Isaiah 65:21-22a).

- As God's people today, we continue to set our sights on the fulfillment of these promises. What are you specifically anticipating when your exile on this broken planet is over?

OLD TESTAMENT *Prophets*

With so many prophets bringing God's messages throughout the Bible, it can be challenging to keep track of where they fall in the biblical timeline. Take a moment to review this chart of some key prophets (though it is not exhaustive), and notice the **country** each prophet's message was directed toward as well as the **kings** who ruled that region. You'll also find the **approximate time period** when each prophet delivered his message from God, whether before, during or after the Babylonian and Assyrian exiles.[24] Finally, the **category** of "major prophet" includes those who wrote lengthy books of the Bible while "minor prophets" had messages shorter in length — though no less important!

PROPHET	COUNTRY	KINGS	*Approx.* TIME PERIOD	CATEGORY
Elijah	Israel	Ahab	ca. 875-850 B.C. (Israel's era of kings)	Early
Elisha	Israel	Joram, Jehu, Jehoahaz, Jehoash	ca. 855-800 B.C. (Israel's era of kings)	Early
Joel	Judah (southern kingdom)	Uncertain	ca. 836-796 B.C. (or some suggest possibly 5th century B.C.)	Pre-exilic minor prophet
Jonah	Assyria	Adad-nirari III, Shalmaneser IV, Ashur-dan III, Ashur-nirari V	ca. 786-746 B.C. (before Assyrian exile)	Pre-exilic minor prophet
Hosea	Israel	Zechariah, Shallum, Menahem, Pekahiah, Pekah, Hoshea	ca. 786-746 B.C. (before Assyrian exile)	Pre-exilic minor prophet
Amos	Israel	Jereboam II, Zechariah, Shallum, Menahem	ca. 760-750 B.C. (before Assyrian exile)	Pre-exilic minor prophet
Isaiah	Judah	Uzziah, Jotham, Ahaz, Hezekiah, Manasseh	ca. 740-698 B.C. (Assyrian exile began in 722)	Pre-exilic major prophet

[24] *The Old Testament Handbook* (Brentwood, TN: Holman Reference, 2023), 123, 239.

PROPHET	COUNTRY	KINGS	*Approx.* TIME PERIOD	CATEGORY
Micah	Judah	Jotham, Ahaz, Hezekiah	ca. 735-710 B.C. (Assyrian exile began in 722)	Pre-exilic minor prophet
Nahum	Assyria	Ashurbanipal	ca. 686-612 B.C. (after Assyrian exile, before Babylonian exile)	Pre-exilic minor prophet
Zephaniah	Judah	Josiah	ca. 640-621 B.C. (before Babylonian exile)	Pre-exilic minor prophet
Jeremiah	Judah	Josiah, Jehoahaz, Jehoiakim, Jehoiachin, and Zedekiah	ca. 627-584 B.C. (Babylonian exile began in 586)	Pre-exilic major prophet
Habakkuk	Judah	Josiah, Jehoahaz, Jehoiakim, Jehoiachin, Zedekiah	ca. 608-598 B.C. (before Babylonian exile)	Pre-exilic minor prophet
Daniel	Exiles in Babylon and Persia	Nebuchadnezzar (Babylon)	6th century B.C. (Babylonian exile)	Exilic major prophet
Ezekiel	Exiles in Babylon	Nebuchadnezzar (Babylon)	ca. 593-571 B.C. (Babylonian exile)	Exilic major prophet
Obadiah	Edom	Uncertain	sometime between 587-500 B.C. (Babylonian exile)	Exilic or post-exilic minor prophet
Haggai	Judah	Cyrus (Persia)	ca. 520 B.C. (some exiles returned from Babylon)	Post-exilic minor prophet
Zechariah	Judah	Cyrus (Persia)	ca. 520-514 B.C. (some exiles returned from Babylon)	Post-exilic minor prophet
Malachi	Judah	Cyrus (Persia)	ca. 500-450 B.C. (some exiles remained in Persia)	Post-exilic minor prophet

day 15 / MALACHI 4:4-6

During 400 years of silence, God's people did not hear new revelation from Him.

When the Jewish exiles finally began to return to Israel from Babylon, they received messages from the Lord through post-exilic prophets, including Haggai, Zechariah and Malachi. Malachi was a contemporary of the prophet Nehemiah, who led the final exiles back from Babylon in 444 B.C.

But after those prophets ceased speaking — during the timespan from Nehemiah to the birth of John the Baptist — came a time often called the "400 years of silence." This refers to the absence of prophets, and therefore the lack of prophetic messages, that came to God's people. This 400-year span separates the end of the Old Testament from the beginning of the New Testament in our Bibles.

- Read Amos 8:11. What type of famine did Amos prophesy, and how did the 400 years of silence fulfill this prophecy?

This was a type of exile from God's revelation. And during these long, silent years, the Jews also faced oppression from Antiochus Epiphanes of Syria. Among many other atrocities, he offered a pig (considered profane by Jewish law [Leviticus 11:7-8]) on the altar in the temple after capturing Jerusalem in 167 B.C. A Jewish family named Maccabeus is credited with leading a revolt, with some success, though the rebellion was eventually quelled and the nation fell to foreign rule once more.

During this time, God wasn't absent from His people's lives, but He wasn't speaking to them as He had in the past; He wasn't sending prophets. Still, the people had the Scriptures that were already written, and the final words of the final prophet in the Old Testament gave a glimpse into God's future plan.

- In Malachi 4:4-6, what did Malachi encourage God's people to "*remember*"?

- Who would God send before the Day of the Lord? What would his purpose be?

After encouraging the people to remember God's commands, Malachi prophesied that the prophet Elijah would return (remember him from Day 12 of our study?).

- Now read Luke 1:13-17, and summarize the fulfillment of Malachi's prophecy in your own words:

John the Baptist, who was filled with God's Spirit and, like Elijah, was a prophet of the Lord, ended God's long silence. He prepared the way for Jesus — the Word of God Himself — to come into the world and dwell with us (John 1:6-14)! Jesus was the true hope for those who had lived through generations of silence, and He is our hope today.

Additionally, Malachi 4:6 promised that God's prophet (John) would *"turn the hearts of fathers to their children and the hearts of children to their fathers."* And we hear echoes of this familial language in Luke 1:16-17, also speaking about John the Baptist: *"He will turn many of the children of Israel to the Lord their God ... the hearts of the fathers to the children ..."* Part of living as exiles on a fallen planet includes complicated relationships, but John's ministry pointed to Christ as the only One who can heal our fractured families. The Old and New Testaments both reveal a healing of family relationships where parents and children are reconciled to one another while also being reconciled to our heavenly Father.

In one sense, we get to experience this healing right now, as God adopts us into His family through our faith in Jesus. We are restored to the Father because the first Christmas, the first coming of Jesus into the world, was the *"day of the Lord"* prophesied in Malachi 4:5. At the same time, there is also a Day of the Lord that is still to come: It will happen when Jesus returns to gather His family to be with Him forever.

While nothing is perfect on this side of heaven, we can seek to turn our faces toward one another as we wait patiently for Jesus' second coming. And we don't have to live in an exile of silence, without hearing God's voice, because we have His completed Scriptures speaking to us any time we choose to listen.

Romans 15:4 says, *"For whatever was written in the past was written for our instruction, so that we may have hope through endurance and through the encouragement from the Scriptures."*
- What scriptures can you call to mind or commit to memory today for encouragement as you await Jesus' return?

WEEK 3 WEEKEND *Video* AND *Prayer*

As we conclude Week 3 of our study together, we're excited to share a video teaching from two experts on the topics of this week's study: Eric Gagnon, Theological Content Manager at Proverbs 31 Ministries, and distinguished Old Testament scholar and professor Dr. Carol Kaminski.

Scan the QR code or visit https://first5.org/video-study to watch Eric's interview with Dr. Kaminski, which explores important questions about this week's scriptures and digs deeper into what we've been learning about exile.

Disclaimer: Links to additional content subject to expiration.

As you watch, feel free to jot down your notes and reflections in the space below — then join us in prayer to wrap up the week.

God, living in exile can feel complicated most days. We long to be with You, but here on earth, we struggle with tasks, problems or people in the Scripture

God, living in exile can feel complicated most days. We long to be with You, but here on earth, we struggle with tasks, problems and people. Thank You for examples from Scripture that encourage and strengthen us. Elijah's food and rest remind us that You supply compassion when we get weary. The way You sent Jesus — the Word made flesh — to break a 400-year silence also reminds us that patiently waiting on You is worthwhile. Show us what it looks like to receive Your grace. Help us to remember that You hold the future. Give us the power to navigate living on earth while our citizenship is in heaven. In Jesus' name, amen.

how did Jesus experience exile

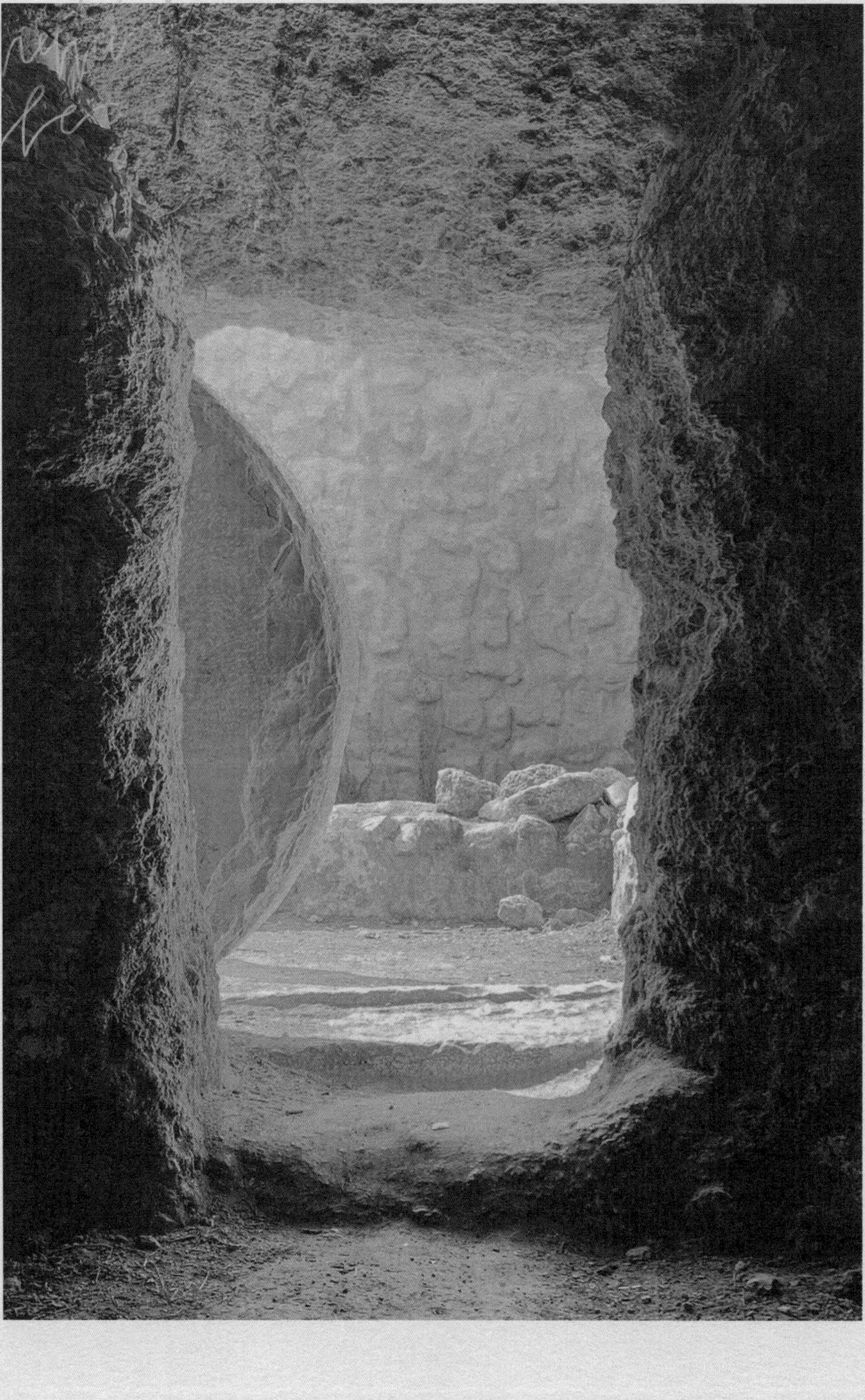

WEEK (*Four*)

HOW DID JESUS EXPERIENCE EXILE?

Introduction

WEEK FOUR

At some point in life, we all face foundational questions about our existence. Often, those points in life end up being times of tension and turmoil. Times when things are shaky and unpredictable. When we truly look at ourselves and wonder:[25]

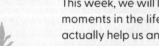

1. **Who are we?**
2. **Where are we?**
3. **What is wrong?**
4. **What is the solution?**

This week, we will look at specific moments in the life of Christ that actually help us answer all of these questions.

Along the way, we'll find that exile was part of the very fabric of Jesus' earthly mission: In fact, His life and ministry are in many ways a retelling of the exile story of Israel. Jesus was tempted just as the Israelites were tempted in the wilderness. But He was faithful where the Israelites, like all of us, were unfaithful.

If you've ever wondered, *Does God actually get what I'm going through? ...* the answer is a resounding yes. That is the magnificence of what theologians call Jesus' "incarnation": Jesus left His glorious home in heaven and took on

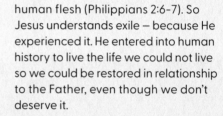

human flesh (Philippians 2:6-7). So Jesus understands exile — because He experienced it. He entered into human history to live the life we could not live so we could be restored in relationship to the Father, even though we don't deserve it.

The book of Hebrews summarizes this powerfully: "*Now since the children have flesh and blood in common, Jesus also shared in these, so that through his death he might destroy the one holding the power of death—that is, the devil—and free those who were held in slavery all their lives by the fear of death*" (Hebrews 2:14-15).

Notice the language of being *"held in slavery"* and *"fear of death."* This is exilic language that reminds us of Adam and Eve's expulsion from their home: the initial separation between humanity and God. What Jesus did in the incarnation — taking on flesh yet remaining fully God, having all things in common with humanity yet remaining sinless — was the key to ending this exile for all who will trust in Him.

Just a few verses later, Hebrews 2:17 tells us Jesus had to become one of us and be made like us in all ways so He could pay the debt we owe God because of our sin. As we work through

[25]These four questions are posed by N.T. Wright. See *The New Testament and the People of God*, (Fortress Press, 1992), 243.

each day of this week's study, we will find that Jesus answers the core questions we wrestle with as a result of our exile:

- **Who are we?** We are created by God to belong in the household of God.
- **Where are we?** In one sense, believers in Jesus are no longer spiritually exiled, but all people live in a sort of exile here on earth because of sin. We are separated from our Father and living outside of our rightful home.
- **What is wrong?** We have no way to get ourselves out of exile on our own.
- **What is the solution?** Jesus lived a sinless life of exile and defeated death through His death and resurrection so that exiles like us can be set free, returning to our Father.

Through faith in Jesus, *"[we] are no longer foreigners and strangers, but fellow citizens with the saints, and members of God's household"* (Ephesians 2:19). This is the Good News, friend! This is how Jesus welcomes us home.

— *Dr. Joel Muddamalle*

day 16 / JOHN 1:1-14

Jesus holds the world together, but the world did not recognize Him.

Have you ever gone someplace where you felt like you didn't belong? How about going somewhere familiar, somewhere you should belong and feel comfortable, but you feel totally out of place – or even worse, rejected? In these situations, you may feel confused and wonder why you have to endure this.

Today's reading in John 1 gives us insight into the incarnation of Christ and how He was not welcomed when He came to earth as God in human form. However, unlike how we might feel confused about our suffering, Jesus *purposely* endured rejection – because He knew it was the only way to save us.

In John 1:1, we get a kind of commentary on the creation story of Genesis 1. John 1:1 tells us *"the Word,"* who we know is Jesus, was *"with God"* and *"was God"* in the beginning, prior to creation.
- And not only was the Word (Jesus) present at creation, but what does John 1:3-5 reveal about how He participated in creation?

With all this in mind, in John 1:11, we get to the tension of the text: Jesus came into the world, but *"his own people did not receive him."*
- What locations, people or situations have left you feeling out of place? What does it mean to you that Jesus personally understands these feelings and had similar experiences?

Notice that with Jesus, we have a reversal of Adam and Eve's story arc:

Adam and Eve were **sent out of Eden** because of **their sin.**
Jesus was **sent out of heaven** to deal with **our sin.**

Jesus didn't do anything wrong – but in obedience to the Father, Jesus was sent into the world for the good of humanity (John 17:18; John 20:21).

John 1:10 says Jesus *"was in the world ... yet the world did not recognize him."* The Greek word for "world" is *kosmos,* and in this context, it refers to "the realm of mankind which, though created by the Word, became alienated from the life of God."[26] All of this language has overtones of exile and separation. Jesus also *"came to **his own"*** according to verse 11 (emphasis added), and the Greek phrase *ta idia* (*"his own"*) is connected to other scriptures that suggest the idea of home. For instance,

[26] William Hendriksen and Simon J. Kistemaker, *Exposition of the Gospel According to John,* vol. 1, New Testament Commentary (Grand Rapids, MI: Baker Book House, 1953-2001), 79-80.

John 19:27 describes how the Apostle John took Mary, the mother of Jesus, to *"his own home"* (ESV).[27]

This deep theology and language work is so important! Jesus was sent by His Father (our Father, God, the King of heaven and earth) to right the wrongs that have plagued humanity since the sin of Genesis 3 left all of us exiled from Eden. Jesus became the bridge to reconnect us to the Father. The incarnation of Jesus was the beginning of the end of our exile — even though many of His own people, His family, rejected Him.

We're going to talk about this more over the next few days, but I want to end today with this: When we wonder if any good could come from our experiences of rejection or feeling like we don't belong … we know that much good came from Jesus' own feelings of exile and loneliness through His incarnation.
  · What does Hebrews 2:15-17 remind us about the purpose of Jesus being exiled from heaven and coming to live on the earth as fully human and fully God?

Jesus understands our pain. Jesus empathizes with the sting of loneliness.

And when we look at His earthly life, we find such kindness and compassion for those who felt like they didn't belong. He talked to a lonely woman at a well (John 4) and healed people who suffered from isolating illnesses (Matthew 9:20-22; Matthew 8:1-3). Have you ever wondered why this is? Jesus understood exactly how it felt to be an outcast. And when we feel something personally, it shapes how we relate to other people.
  · What would it look like practically for you to receive comfort from Jesus in the midst of trials or rejection? How could you then offer His comfort and love to others?

It may be hard to hear that your feelings of loneliness and rejection can be used for good. But Jesus shows us that just because it's hard doesn't mean it's not true. Today, friend, you can lay your head down with this simple but profound assurance: Jesus knows, and He understands. He gets it. And that's one of the most comforting truths we can receive.

---

[27] William Hendriksen and Simon J. Kistemaker. Note: *οἱ ἴδιοι* means "those of his own home," cf. 13:1.

"Adopt the same attitude as that of Christ Jesus, who, existing in the form of God, did not consider equality with God as something to be exploited. Instead he emptied himself by assuming the form of a servant, taking on the likeness of humanity. And when he had come as a man, he humbled himself by becoming obedient to the point of death—even to death on a cross."

PHILIPPIANS 2:5-8

day 17 / MATTHEW 2:13-21

As a child, Jesus escaped to Egypt for safety, though He would later return home to Israel.

Sometimes, the hardest situations we are forced to live through end up being the very places where God shows up unexpectedly to secure comfort for us. Early in the life of Jesus, our Savior was already proving this to be true.

Things were filled with turmoil: After three wise men visited young Jesus and His earthly parents, Mary and Joseph, an angel of the Lord spoke to Joseph and told him to *"flee to Egypt"* (Matthew 2:13). The reigning Jewish king, Herod, was jealous of King Jesus and gave an order to kill all male children 2 years old or younger. Under cover of darkness, Joseph took Mary and Jesus and withdrew to Egypt.

In other words, they went into exile. And it wasn't until after Herod died that Joseph received another dream from the Lord letting him know it was safe for the family to return to Israel (Matthew 2:19-21).

So things ended up OK for Jesus. Because of this, we may be tempted to move on from this story quickly, but I want us to pause and really reflect on what took place. Remember: There is always reason for repetition in Scripture. And the more closely we study the narrative of Scripture, the more we realize there are echoes we are meant to hear.

Let's look at some of these echoes by comparing some of the significant figures and places in Jesus' story to similar figures and places in the Old Testament:

Old TESTAMENT	*New* TESTAMENT
Jacob's son **Joseph** received a **dream from the Lord** and brought his family – who became the nation of Israel – **to Egypt** for safety.	Jesus' father, **Joseph**, received a **dream from the Lord** and acted on that dream to save his family, which happened to take them **to Egypt.**
Pharaoh ordered the murder of Jewish male babies in Egypt. God saved one **innocent** child, Moses, and set him apart to **rescue** the Israelite nation.	**Herod ordered the murder of Jewish boys** in an attempt to kill the Savior of God's people. Jesus would later give His **innocent** life to eternally **rescue** believers from every nation.
Egypt was a temporary sanctuary for the Israelites during years of famine but later became a land of exile and slavery, so God led them **out of Egypt.**	**Egypt became a temporary sanctuary** for Jesus and His family as they ran for their lives. Jesus then had to come **out of Egypt** to return home to the land of promise.
Once rescued out of Egypt, God's children were on their way home to the promised land, but they were **unfaithful** and experienced punishment and judgment for their sins.	When Jesus returned home to Israel, He lived a life of **perfect faithfulness** that ultimately led Him to the cross, where He vanquished sin and death forever.

- As you study today's Bible passage and the chart above, what similarities stand out to you the most between Jesus' journey and Israel's journey? Do you see any additional similarities?

- How do Matthew 2:15 and verses 17-18 also connect today's scriptures to the Old Testament? (Hint: Look up Hosea 11:1 and Jeremiah 31:15-16.)

There are many more parallel details too. Joseph took his family and left *"during the night"* (Matthew 2:14), which echoes Exodus 12:31, where Pharaoh told Moses and his brother Aaron to leave Egypt *"during the night."* [28] This is truly mind-blowing!

Through all of this, we find Jesus reliving the life of Israel. New Testament scholar N.T. Wright says, "Exile and restoration was the central drama that Israel believed itself to be acting out. Jesus belongs exactly within that drama."[29] Jesus was not only "within" the drama, but He was actually reenacting it — yet where Israel proved to be faithless, Jesus would always be faithful.
- What new perspectives or understandings of Jesus' life and ministry do you find when you consider how He reenacted and redeemed Israel's story of exile?

Tucked away in all of this is another surprising comfort: At the time Jesus and His family escaped from Bethlehem in Israel and fled to Egypt, historians estimate there was likely a large Jewish population there. Imagine leaving everything you knew in a hurry, having no idea what you'd find in Egypt, but then seeing that smack in the middle of an unfamiliar land, there were people who shared your faith in God.

In the next few weeks, we are going to talk more about the Church as God's family, but I want to just say right here that part of God's kindness is to offer us community and belonging with fellow believers in Him. No church is perfect — but still, the family of God is where all those who belong to Jesus can also find belonging with one another.
- As you imagine Jesus' family and community in Egypt, how might this give you hope for finding community in God's family today?

---

[28] Craig S. Keener, *The IVP Bible Background Commentary: New Testament* (Downers Grove, IL: InterVarsity Press, 1993), Matthew 2:13-14.

[29] James M. Scott, *Exile: A Conversation with N.T. Wright* (Downers Grove, IL: IVP Academic, 2017), 45.

day 18 / MATTHEW 4:1-11

Jesus was tempted in the wilderness and was faithful and obedient to God.

A pivotal moment in many of our lives is when we move out of our childhood home. Whether we move out for college, a job, marriage or some other adventure, if the experiences we had in our childhood home were positive, it usually only takes a little time before homesickness settles in. We might miss the familiar sound of family moving in the house. The favorite pet that annoyed us to death, but now we would do anything to have him near us again. The food and the smells.

If we can't be home, the next best thing is often to bring parts of home to ourselves. This may mean finding some home-style foods or grabbing a candle with a fragrance that reminds us of our family. These little things, when we are far away from home, can truly sustain us.

So what sustains the people of God in exile?

Today we'll find out by looking at Matthew 4:1-11. It's an epic scene where Jesus spiritually did battle with the devil in the wilderness.

- What stands out to you from Jesus' responses to Satan in this wilderness account? How does Jesus' response to temptation compare to other biblical figures we've studied (for instance, Adam and Eve, Jacob, Joseph, Israel's kings)?

Remember that this week we are looking at how parts of Jesus' life mirrored the journey of Israel in the Old Testament — and a massive part of Israel's story involved 40 years of wandering in the wilderness.

When Israel first escaped the tyranny of Pharaoh and went into the wilderness, God led them in a pillar of cloud by day and fire by night (Exodus 13:21). With this in mind, let's look at how Jesus ended up in the wilderness.

- According to Matthew 4:1, who led Jesus into the wilderness?

The devil wasn't ultimately in charge here. The Holy Spirit was. And the wilderness, as we've mentioned, was a place rich with meaning and history for God's people.

The wilderness was known for three things: [30]

[30] Grant R. Osborne, *Matthew*, vol. 1, Zondervan Exegetical Commentary on the New Testament (Grand Rapids, MI: Zondervan, 2010), 131.

1. It was a place where evil spirits were said to reside (Isaiah 13:21; Isaiah 34:14).[31]

2. It was a place where Israel's faith was tested (Deuteronomy 8:2).

3. It was a place where God's people received comfort (1 Kings 19:4–8).

In the wilderness, after fasting for 40 days (parallel to Israel's 40 years), Jesus faced temptation, but He was faithful to God in all the ways Israel was unfaithful. Jesus quoted three Scripture passages as His response to the devil: Each of these passages was from Deuteronomy, and they were all commandments that Israel had failed to obey.[32]

- How does Matthew 4:3-4 highlight Jesus' faithfulness in comparison to Israel's unfaithfulness in Exodus 16:2-3?

- How does Matthew 4:9-10 highlight Jesus' faithfulness in comparison to Israel's unfaithfulness in Judges 2:11-12?

In the wilderness …

1. Jesus won an important victory over evil forces — in this case, the devil himself.

2. Jesus acted in obedience to the commandments of God and passed the test Israel was unable to pass.

3. Jesus received divine comfort from the Father (Matthew 4:11).

How was Jesus able to do this? The answer is simple, but it is far from simplistic. Jesus went to the comfort of Scripture. He refused to be derailed or sidetracked by pride but in humility referred to God's Word.

- How have the Scriptures sustained you during wilderness seasons in your life, or how could you turn to Scripture for this purpose today? If any specific passages come to mind, list them below.

In John 1:1, we saw that Jesus is the very Word of God. Here in His wilderness temptation, the *living Word of God actually lived out the Word of God* to perfection. While Jesus was in the wilderness, He turned to the Scriptures to sustain Him.

As we live out our faith and wait patiently for the second coming of Christ, we, too, can meditate on the Scriptures. In our longing for our eternal home, we can catch a glimpse and foretaste of the goodness of the new heaven and new earth as we steep our hearts in the Word of God. The Scriptures sustained Jesus, and they can do the same for us today.

---

[31] The Hebrew words translated into "*wild goats*" in Isaiah 13:21 and "*night bird*" in Isaiah 34:14 (literally "Lillith") are actually references to evil spirits from common folklore during that time. Interestingly, Jesus seems to confirm that evil spirits really do "*roam*" dry, wilderness-like "*waterless places*" (Matthew 12:43).

[32] Craig S. Keener, *Matthew*, vol. 1, The IVP New Testament Commentary Series (Downers Grove, IL: InterVarsity Press, 1997), Matthew 4:1-11.

In His human nature, Jesus experienced true and total exile on the cross.

There used to be an old show called *Are You Afraid of the Dark?* The whole point of the show was to scare people — and what scares people more than the dark? In the darkness, we can't see. And for those of us who have the ability to see, losing that ability often means losing our sense of control. If we don't have control, we feel vulnerable. And to be vulnerable is to be open to being hurt.

In Matthew 27:45-46, we enter the darkest, most painful day in human history. This was the day when Jesus, the perfect Son of God, gave up His life for us on the cross. But interestingly, it is also known as Good Friday — because even in Jesus' crucifixion, *"the darkness did not overcome"* (John 1:5).

· What details does Matthew 27:45 give us regarding darkness on the day Jesus died? How was this darkness both literal and symbolic?

· What areas of your life feel dark today, and how might this allow you to relate to today's Bible passage or *"share in the sufferings of Christ"* (1 Peter 4:13)?

In the midst of darkness, Jesus cried out loud a plea to the Father: *"'Elí, Elí, lemá sabachtháni?' that is, 'My God, my God, why have you abandoned me?'"* (Matthew 27:46).

It may be hard to imagine, but Jesus was truly abandoned on the cross as He took on the sins of humanity and secured victory for us through His self-sacrifice.

Previously, Jesus had also been abandoned and hurt by people throughout His earthly life. In fact, the days leading up to His crucifixion were filled with hard experiences for Jesus:

1. Jesus was abandoned by His disciples (Matthew 26:56).
2. Jesus was denied by Peter (Matthew 26:69-75).
3. Jesus was condemned by religious leaders (Matthew 26:57-68).
4. Jesus was rejected by His own people in Israel (Matthew 27:15-26).
5. Jesus was ridiculed by Roman soldiers (Matthew 27:27-31).

You may be sitting in a situation right now that is hard. You may feel like, around the corner, something is waiting to create even more disappointment in your life. Jesus also walked through the reality of abandonment, and He felt the depth of the deepest pain of exile: separation from God.

- Yet in this moment on the cross, Jesus again drew on Scripture. What words do you find in Psalm 22:1, and how does this relate to Matthew 27:46?

On the cross, by quoting an Old Testament psalm, Jesus placed His own story squarely in the context of Israel's story from the Old Testament. On the cross, we could say Jesus "began the end" of the spiritual exile of sin. Jesus made a way for God's people to return to Eden and experience the fullness of His Kingdom on the earth.

- How have you seen the Lord work in your life through hard experiences? How might you gain spiritual perspective by placing your own story in the context of God's larger redemptive plan?

On the cross, Jesus was victorious, not defeated. And when He resurrected three days later, He proved He had triumphed over death forever.

This victory of Jesus makes possible our reconciliation to God. Jesus repairs the relationship between God and His creation that was ruptured by sin in Genesis 3 — including the relationship between God and people and relationships between people themselves. For all who will trust in Him, Jesus has ended our spiritual exile and opened the way for us to live in intimate relationship with the Father, through the Son, equipped and empowered by the Spirit.

- As you consider Jesus' sacrifice, write a prayer of thanks to the Lord for how He has ended your spiritual exile:

I love how the Apostle Paul later summarized all of this:

"Death has been swallowed up in victory. Where, death, is your victory? Where, death, is your sting? The sting of death is sin, and the power of sin is the law. But thanks be to God, who gives us the victory through our Lord Jesus Christ!" (1 Corinthians 15:55-57).

Today, when you consider the cross and the empty tomb, you can know with assurance that for every believer in Jesus, our spiritual exile is over.

day 20 / ACTS 1:4-11

Jesus returned home to heaven and took His rightful place at the right hand of the Father.

We started this week talking about the miracle of the *incarnation*: God taking on flesh to be with us (John 1:14). Let's end our week talking about the glory of the *ascension* of Jesus back to heaven after His resurrection.

The ascension of Christ may tragically be one of the most neglected doctrines, or teachings, of the Church. You may often hear the work of Jesus summarized as His "death, burial and resurrection." But what about His ascension? If the cross ended the spiritual exile of all believers in Jesus, His ascension ushered in the beginning of the end of our physical exile: While we currently live on earth, the ascension of Jesus promises we will dwell with Him in eternity. For now, we wait patiently for the return of Christ, the victorious King of heaven and earth.

Unfortunately, waiting can be hard. In today's society, new products (phones, tablets, computers, cars, appliances) promise to make our lives easy by offering speed and efficiency. No need to wait in line for food — just use an app. Don't worry about chasing down an answer to a question — just type it into a search bar.
  · What are some thoughts, actions or feelings that often surface when you have to wait on something in your life?

  · Do you feel similar emotions (annoyance, restlessness, discontentment, etc.) about waiting for Jesus' return? Why or why not?

The world often promises speed, but throughout Scripture, we are called to patience:

Patience to endure suffering (Romans 8:18; Romans 8:23-25).
Patience to wait on the provision of God (1 Timothy 6:17).
Patience to experience the goodness God has in store for us (Romans 8:28).

Patience is a powerful spiritual discipline that many of us have underdeveloped. And patience is exactly what Jesus called His disciples to as He ascended to the right hand of the Father. Acts 1:4a tells us Jesus commanded the disciples to *"wait for the Father's promise."* Waiting and patience have a purpose.
  · Read Romans 5:3-5, and list some of the good work the Lord can do during difficult times in our lives:

Waiting patiently teaches us perseverance. It forms us into the image of Christ, a process referred to theologically as "sanctification." This sets us up to live as faithful citizens of the Kingdom of God even while we remain *"strangers and exiles"* in a land that is not our final home (1 Peter 2:11).

This context is important when we study the ascension of Jesus. In Acts 1:7-8, Jesus said:

"It is not for you to know times or periods that the Father has set by his own authority. But you will receive power when the Holy Spirit has come on you, and you will be my witnesses in Jerusalem, in all Judea and Samaria, and to the ends of the earth."

With Jesus' ascension comes a renewed commision for us to be His witnesses *"to the ends of the earth."* Your ears may be ringing right now as you remember God's original mandate to Adam and Eve …
  · Let's review: What did God tell Adam and Eve (humanity) to do in Genesis 1:28?

Jesus restores our relationship with the Father, putting us back on the trajectory humanity was always supposed to be on — faithfully bearing witness to the Father and spreading the image of God to the ends of the earth. The physical ascension of Christ leaves the people of God as "necessary witnesses" on earth, as we are now the primary means of communicating the goodness of Christ to the world.[33]
  · How does 2 Corinthians 5:18-21 echo this commission?

God makes His appeal to the world in and through us. Why? Because Christ desires for the world to return from spiritual exile into intimate union with the Father.

This means you and I have a purpose to fulfill as we wait patiently for our homecoming. We don't wait without purpose but rather with eager anticipation that leads us to share the gospel with the world.

The Christ who ascended will return, and when He does, He will establish the new heaven and new earth. This is when our exile will truly and fully end. The people of God will be with God forever. And until then, we are agents of redemption for God to work through as He calls His people to Himself.
  · Who can you pray for and share the love of Christ with this week? How might it motivate you to share the gospel when you consider that those who don't know Jesus are still living in spiritual exile?

This calling can feel so daunting and massive! But let's simplify it. If you are wondering how in the world to start … you can be a faithful witness of Jesus in the carpool line as you show kindness to teachers and other parents. Or through conversations that come up with neighbors as you process life together. It can be in your workplace as you look for opportunities both to live the gospel and to share it with co-workers. It is part of raising your children to know and love Jesus. All of these activities, and so many more, bring about a type of redemption of our exilic lives. And we can start right where we are.

[33] Peter C. Orr, *Exalted above the Heavens: The Risen and Ascended Christ*, ed. D. A. Carson, vol. 47, New Studies in Biblical Theology (Downers Grove, IL; London: IVP Academic: An Imprint of InterVarsity Press; Apollos, 2018), 90.

WEEK 4 WEEKEND *Video* AND *Prayer*

As we conclude Week 4 of our study together, we're excited to share another video teaching from the writer of this week's study, Dr. Joel Muddamalle.

Scan the QR code or visit https://first5.org/video-study to access Joel's video, where he'll share more insights about this week's scriptures and dig deeper into what we've been learning about exile.

Disclaimer: Links to additional content subject to expiration.

As you watch, feel free to jot down your notes and reflections in the space below — then join us in prayer to wrap up the week.

God, thank You for Your Son, Jesus, who willingly experienced exile from His home in heaven to come and live a perfect, sacrificial life on earth for us. Thank You for Your great love for us, Your children, that You would send Christ to end our exile. I am so grateful for Jesus being faithful in all the ways Israel was unfaithful — and in all the ways I have been unfaithful. Thank You, God, that You are working in me to help me live as a faithful citizen of the Kingdom of God as I await the return of Jesus alongside all my fellow believers across the world. In Jesus' name, amen.

how do we
find community
in exile?

WEEK (*Five*)

HOW DO WE FIND COMMUNITY IN EXILE?

Introduction

WEEK FIVE

Since the start of our study, we have seen how exile can bring out the worst and best in us. Any time we feel uprooted, stress and tension abound. We long to settle in a place of safety and belonging ... but sometimes we seek the wrong things to provide familiarity, comfort or peace.

This week, we'll take a closer look at how believers in Jesus — collectively, the Church — find our spiritual home in Christ though we live as strangers in a world that doesn't know Him. The feeling of unsettledness in this world can be overwhelming. We know the new heaven and earth await us, and this gives us great hope, but it sometimes also makes the waiting hard. We may be tempted to grumble. Worry. Complain. Fear. But what we'll learn is that there is a better way to wait.

Together.

So we choose to wait well. This kind of waiting on the Lord — not passively but actively and obediently — is what God's people were meant to learn in the wilderness so long ago. It's what they were learning during the Assyrian and Babylonian exiles. It's what they were still learning during the Roman occupation in the New Testament. It is the very waiting that you and I are meant to learn today.

How do we learn this type of patient but active waiting?

We gather. We worship. We study God's Word. We go. We pray. We serve. We give. We receive. We suffer together, and we celebrate together. We turn away from sin. We share the message of the gospel, clothed with power and fueled by the Spirit. We honor God. We respect others. We point each other to the One we follow.

We share with others how God wants to lead them out of exile and into His forever family. We partner in building God's Kingdom — not only as a place we will someday inhabit but as a Kingdom where we already have citizenship today (Philippians 1:27).

Questions like "where do I belong?" and "how much longer?" may linger on our lips as we wait for the fullness of His Kingdom. But this beautiful Church family God has created, where we find belonging with our brothers and sisters in Christ, assures us that our perseverance and the mission we are entrusted with — right here and right now — is worth it all.

— *Jenny Wheeler*

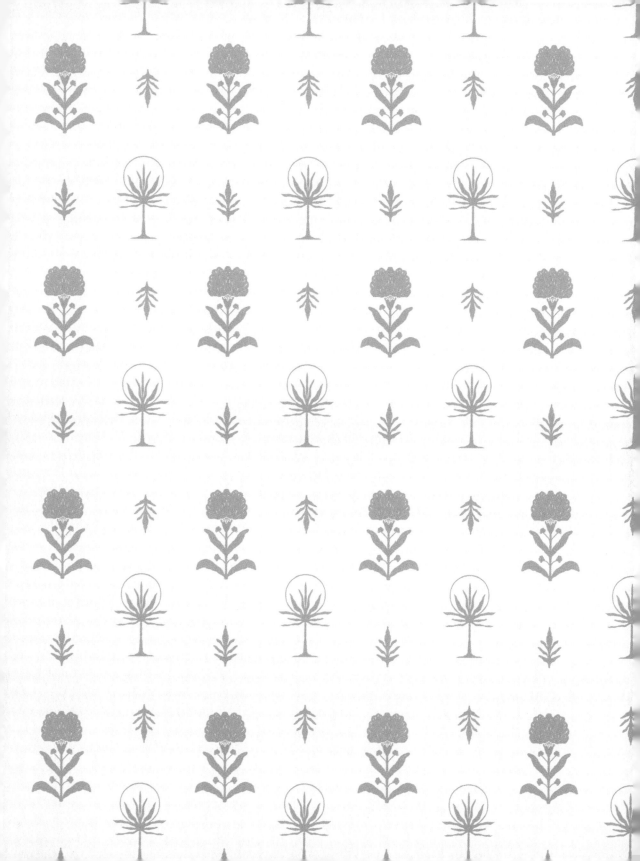

day 21 / ACTS 2

Pentecost reunited exiles and launched the Church.

Last week, we saw that in Acts 1:4, Jesus instructed His disciples to wait in Jerusalem for *"the Father's promise"* of the Holy Spirit. This is the same Spirit we saw *"hovering over the surface of the waters"* in Genesis 1:2, and throughout the Old Testament, God prophesied that He would one day send His Spirit to dwell in the hearts of all believers (Ezekiel 11:19; Isaiah 32:15; Isaiah 44:3).

· According to Joel 2:28-29, who would receive the gift of the Holy Spirit? How would the Holy Spirit empower them?

· Read John 14:16-17a and verse 26. What title(s) did John give the Holy Spirit? What comfort does this give you as a follower of Christ?

God sent the long-awaited Helper to His people at Pentecost, 50 days after Jesus had risen from the grave. *"The day of Pentecost"* (Acts 2:1) was a Jewish festival, also known as the Feast of Weeks or Shavuot, observed annually in Jerusalem seven weeks after Passover. Following Old Testament law, Jewish exiles (those who didn't live in Israel) made the pilgrimage to join their people in Jerusalem to celebrate (Exodus 34:22). Acts 2:9-11 lists more than a dozen places they came from, all with different languages, customs and cultures.

During Pentecost, the Jewish population in the city typically doubled or tripled, which created a uniquely diverse audience for the extraordinary experience found in Acts 2.[34]

Empowered by the Holy Spirit, Jesus' apostles suddenly declared the praises of God in languages that were not their native tongue, yet these dialects were clearly understood by many listeners (Acts 2:8; Acts 2:11). Peter then humbly and boldly preached the first sermon of the New Testament to the amazed crowd gathered near the temple (vv. 14-36).

· In the past, Peter had denied knowing Jesus (you can read about his experience in Mark 14:67 72). But now he confidently shared the message of salvation. How does Peter's transformation encourage us as we live out our faith?

[34] Iain M. Duguid, *ESV Expository Commentary (Volume 9): John–Acts* (Crossway, 2019).

Notably, biblical scholars also refer to Pentecost as a redemptive reversal of what happened at the tower of Babel, which we studied on Day 5.

- Let's recall some of the details here: Why did God disperse the people and create new languages at Babel, according to Genesis 11:5-9?

Driven by a spirit of idolatry and the desire to make a name for themselves, the people at Babel were scattered and sent into exile. Their *selfish spirit* created *separation*.

On Pentecost, God gathered descendants of the nations that formed after the tower of Babel, and through the gospel of Christ and the outpouring of the *Holy Spirit,* He *brought together* diverse people. The cultural and ethnic divisions caused by the confusion of languages at Babel no longer separated God's people; they were now reunited through faith in Jesus.

The Holy Spirit transformed exiles who were once *"far off"* (Acts 2:39) into a family of believers. How astounding to see what the Spirit can do through just a few humble and obedient disciples – in one day, the Church family grew by at least 3,000 (v. 41)!

- Acts 2:46-47 and Acts 9:31 note important qualities of the early Church, filled with the Holy Spirit. List those qualities below, and note some specific ways they demonstrate a reversal of exile for God's people.

As we've seen in our study, exile includes separation, pain, and at times what feels like aimless wandering. We face many of the same experiences as we wait for Jesus to return and bring us to our eternal home. But if we are in Christ, we belong to God's family. Today, the people of God are His temple – not a building made by human hands but a living body, fashioned to share in the joy of reconciling others back to Him (1 Corinthians 3:16-17).

NATIONS IN JERUSALEM AT *Pentecost*

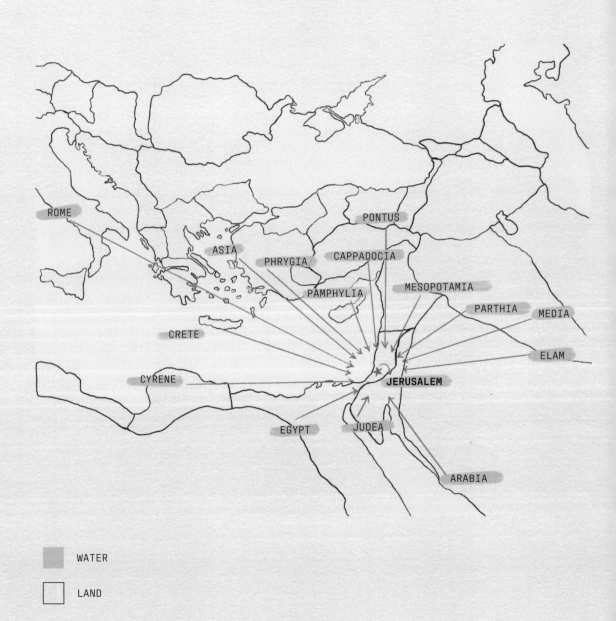

ROME

PONTUS

ASIA

PHRYGIA

CAPPADOCIA

PAMPHYLIA

MESOPOTAMIA

PARTHIA

MEDIA

CRETE

ELAM

CYRENE

JERUSALEM

EGYPT

JUDEA

ARABIA

WATER

LAND

A CHURCH WITH *No Walls*

The New Testament shows us the Church is an integral part of God's plan to reach those who are lost or exiled — sinful humans like you and me — and to reconcile us back to God. Ephesians 5:25-27 says Jesus laid down His life for the Church. Romans 12:5 says that in the Church, *"We who are many are one body in Christ and individually members of one another."* The Church mattered then, and it still matters today.

In Acts 2, several defining characteristics were evident among believers in the early Church, which we also seek to embody today.

The Church is called to:

1. Praise and glorify God.
2. Equip believers and help one another grow spiritually.
3. Share the gospel with the world.

ACTS 2:42	*"They devoted themselves to the apostles' teaching ..."*
ACTS 2:42	*"They devoted themselves to ... fellowship, to the breaking of bread"* and connection with other believers.
ACTS 2:42	*"They devoted themselves to ... prayer."*
ACTS 2:43	*"Everyone was filled with awe"* of God.
ACTS 2:44	Believers dwelled in unity *"together and held all things in common."*
ACTS 2:45	Believers exhibited generosity and met the needs of others *"as any had need."*
ACTS 2:46	They gathered regularly to worship in large groups (*"in the temple"*) and small groups (*"house to house"*).
ACTS 2:47	They offered praise and thanks to God for all of His blessings.
ACTS 2:47	They *"enjoy[ed] the favor of all the people,"* including both believers and those outside of the Church.
ACTS 2:47	They engaged in evangelism as *"every day the Lord added to their number those who were being saved."*

While local gatherings of believers today may exhibit these characteristics in different ways, in different seasons or to varying degrees, the global Church — one with no walls — honors and blesses God, builds the faith of believers, and invites others into community and relationship with Christ. What a gift!

day 22 / ACTS 15:1-20

The early Church gathered, addressed conflict, and established principles for unity during the Council at Jerusalem.

As daughters and sons of God, we have faith in Jesus as the One who unites us. But in God's family, distinctions still exist between individuals and groups, so there will also be opportunities for disagreement or simply differences among believers. The process of loving one another well as a family is good, messy and holy work.

· Consider Jesus' prayer in John 17:20-23. What are we called to seek? What did He say would be the effect?

· According to Ephesians 4:1-3, what qualities does a Christian exhibit?

How we handle tensions that arise is critical to establishing peace and maintaining unity in God's family. By Acts 15, the family of Jewish and gentile (non-Jewish) Christ followers had grown exponentially and rather quickly, which brought the Church its first major theological controversy.

Ephesians 2:12 explains that gentiles were once *"without Christ, excluded from the citizenship of Israel, and foreigners to the covenants of promise, without hope and without God in the world."* But Jesus opened the door to allow gentiles to join God's family through faith in Him (Acts 14:27). Sparks of controversy then arose over the central issue of whether gentiles who followed Jesus also needed to follow the law of the Old Testament as a prerequisite for salvation. Was faith in Christ alone really enough to end their exile?

The spirit of unity from Acts 2 was put to the test in this heated discussion.

· The Apostle Paul, Barnabas and others were sent to Jerusalem to meet with church elders on this matter. What does their example teach us about how to navigate disunity or confusion? What attitudes or actions in Acts 15:6-20 could we emulate today when conflict arises?

The issue essentially boiled down to how sinners can become accepted by God: through our upholding of His law or through our faith in Christ, who fulfilled the law for us.

- According to Matthew 5:17-18, what was Jesus' mission?

- Review Peter's speech in Acts 15:7-11. How did he explain the way we are saved?

Because Jesus fulfilled the law by living a perfect life, law-based rituals like circumcision do not save us. We are saved by grace through faith in Christ.

The Jerusalem Council in Acts 15 thus created a path for gentile and Jewish believers to live in harmony and established that reliance upon God's grace is necessary for healthy conflict resolution (1 Peter 3:8; 1 Corinthians 1:10).

Matthew Henry's commentary describes how the Jerusalem Council relates to us today: "There is a strange proneness in us to think that all do wrong who do not just as we do."[35] In other words, we tend to judge people just for being different from us. But in Christ, we can celebrate that differences exist in this beautiful and diverse family of God. We do not all think the same or do things the same way. Handling our differences with grace, wisdom and reliance on the Spirit — without minimizing Truth and without making allowances for any form of disobedience to God — is what matters.

Early Church leaders modeled this by warning about the dangers of divisiveness, confusion, and viewing personal preferences as more important than God's Truth (Acts 15:19). Being part of the family of Christ and living by the Spirit's leadership enables us to seek the best for others as we all submit to the Lordship of Christ and obey His Word.

When we preserve unity and exercise grace within our churches, a bunch of exiles from all walks of life and backgrounds come together as one good, messy and holy family — the family Jesus gave His life to save.

[35] Henry, M., & Thomas, S. (1981). *Matthew Henry's Concise Commentary on the Whole Bible*. Moody Publishers.

day 23 / HEBREWS 10:22-25

The exiles were instructed to gather and were taught how to live while facing persecution.

The book of Hebrews can be summed up in two major themes: the supremacy of Christ and the call to stay faithful to Him in the face of hardship. As a letter of encouragement originally addressed to Jewish Christians who were ostracized and persecuted for their faith, Hebrews is a message to the Church about how to persevere in a hostile environment.

In light of the looming possibility of martyrdom, feelings of fear and a desire for self-preservation were at an all-time high among Jewish Christians when Hebrews was written. Many were physically displaced or exiled from their homes in Jerusalem because of persecution. Some had stopped sharing the gospel openly.[36] Because their confidence was shaken, some had also withdrawn from the local church gathering, creating another layer of exile or separation.
- Read Hebrews 10:19-22. What is the foundation of a Christian's confidence or *"boldness"*? Based on this foundation, do you think it's possible to be confident and bold even in exile? Why or why not?

Though faithful, gospel-centered community was foundational to the Church in Acts 2, some believers now sought to avoid it. But the writer of Hebrews wanted to remind these exiles that while pulling away from the Church family may have seemed wise during turbulent times, it actually wasn't.

How could this tension and their understandable fears be overcome?
- Let's look at Hebrews 10:23. Fill in the missing words from this passage:

"Let us _____ on to the _____ of our _____ without _____, since he who _____ is _____."

The exiles were reminded to cling to God as their hope and anchor, not to their lives or to the acceptance of this world. He was their source of provision. He was their refuge of protection. And the message of salvation in Him was — and is — worth sharing.
- Think of a time when you've shared your faith with someone open and receptive to God, or consider someone in your life now with whom you could share your faith. What might that interaction do in their life and yours?

[36] R. Kent Hughes, *Hebrews: An Anchor for the Soul (2 volumes in 1 / ESV Edition),* Preaching the Word (Crossway, 2015).

Much like the early Church experienced hardships, so will we. Persecution will come. We will face trials. But we do not lose heart — and we do not stand alone. Rather, we stand together, anchored in God through faith in Christ and filled with the power of His Spirit.

In some cases, there are certainly valid reasons for leaving a particular church or taking a temporary break from gathering in person, but Hebrews 10:25 advises us not to make a *"habit"* of *"neglecting"* church participation altogether. Life will offer us reasons to stay away from church, hide our faith, run from adversity, or pull away from the family of God when conflict or hard times arise. Yet verses 22-25 list three things that would help the first-century Church in exile to stick together, and they can help us as well:

1. **"*Draw near*" to God with sincere hearts through prayer and study of the Word (v. 22).** When we get into the Word, the Word gets into us and comes alive in our hearts. This grows our faith and deepens our understanding of who God is and who He made us to be.

2. **"*Hold on*" tightly to our hope in Jesus (v. 23).** Our hope is not anchored in people, places or things: It's anchored in the work of Jesus on the cross. Though circumstances in our lives may shift, we have a firm and unshakeable foundation (Ephesians 2:20). We are secure in Him, whatever comes and whatever goes.

3. **Devote ourselves to the corporate Church as we "*provoke love*" and "*encourag[e] each other*" in expressions of faith (vv. 24-25).** Our lives are meant to be a blessing and an example to the world. We need each other to carry out this purpose. How we love, give, share, encourage, worship — everything we do — speaks volumes about the God we believe in and serve.

· As we end our time together today, consider the three areas of obedience listed above. Which do you find the easiest? Which is the most difficult? Ask your faithful God to help you. He is more than able.

WHAT THE CHURCH WEARS: *Let's Get Dressed*

Written as a letter from the Apostle Paul to the churches of Colossae and nearby Laodicea, the book of Colossians warns about the dangers of false prophets and straying from the Truth. In Colossians 3:8-17, Paul reminded believers how to live and treat one another within the context of the local church family.

Let's look at Colossians 3:8. Fill in the blanks for what to get rid of or lay aside:

"But now, put away all the following: anger, _____, _____, _____, and filthy _____ from your _____."

For those whose lives are now hidden in Christ (v. 4), living the old way, according to the flesh, is not truly living.

So Paul encouraged the believers, in Colossians 3:12-13, to *"put on"* new spiritual clothes:

"Therefore, as God's chosen ones, holy and dearly loved, put on _____ , _____, humility, _____, and _____ , bearing with one another and _____ one another ... Just as the Lord has forgiven you, so you are also to _____."

It all starts with the heart. Therefore, in verse 14, Paul listed one thing that is most important of all. The one thing that creates harmony and binds everything together: **love.**

For the early Church and for us today, our faith is most fully exercised and realized in community, even as we also grow individually through God's work in our own hearts. When we put on the spiritual garments that cultivate care and build up others in the Church family, we further the cause of Christ in a lost world. How we treat others both within and outside of the Church is a reflection of God's Spirit within us. His love shining through us will never go out of style and will point others to Him (John 13:35).

day 24 / 1 PETER 2:11-17

Exiled Christians learned what it meant to live honorably and humbly within the community and before others.

Our Scripture reading on Day 21 this week showed us how Peter was an instrumental leader in the early Church. Peter's message in today's passage presents several more truths that also apply powerfully to the Church today:

1. Peter highlighted how balanced respect for authority, knowing that God is the true King of all, is key to living a life of godliness (vv. 13-16).
2. Peter also pointed out that honorable, good conduct can point others to Christ in the midst of a fallen world (vv. 11-12).

In 1 Peter 2:11, Peter referred to the Church using the terms *"strangers and exiles,"* but he wasn't talking about believers being spiritually separated from God. Becoming a part of God's family changes the nature of our exile: Instead of being spiritually exiled from God's presence because of our sin, we are now spiritually united with God, yet we are *"strangers"* to the sinful world.

Still, we don't live with an attitude of hostility toward the world — even though the world may be hostile toward us.

- According to today's passage, what are some ways God enables us to honor authority, truly love others, and fear Him with holy reverence even in a world that doesn't follow Him?

As aliens and strangers awaiting Jesus' return to fully inaugurate God's Kingdom in the new heaven and new earth, the people of God live in the tension of two different powers: powers of this world (governments and leaders) and the power of God.

Especially for the Jewish exiles Peter was originally addressing, living under Roman authority required submission, or deference out of common respect.[37] Yet Peter was also clear that a believer's primary allegiance and affection are directed toward God. In verse 17, Peter said it is proper both to *"honor the emperor"* and to *"fear God"* — the first out of respect for authority, the second out of holy reverence.

Daniel, an Old Testament prophet, modeled this well when he was an exile in Babylon. Under the rule of the worldly King Nebuchadnezzar, Daniel chose not to defile himself with foods that were presumably unclean according to the law of God (Daniel 1:8). Daniel's respectful request reflected His reverence for God even while living under a human ruler who did not fear Him.

[37] J. Ramsey Michaels, *Word Biblical Themes: 1 Peter* (Zondervan Academic, 2020).

- According to Daniel 1:9 and Daniel 1:17, what blessings did Daniel receive from God as a result of his faithfulness? What do 1 Peter 2:15 and 1 Peter 2:12 say will result from our faithful obedience to God today?

Affirming what we learn from Daniel in the Old Testament, Peter emphasized in the New Testament that our identity and allegiance are to be found solely in Christ, no matter where we call "home" on earth. **How** we live is more important than **where** we live. And because of that, a true follower of Christ seeks to act honorably before God and people.

- Look back at 1 Peter 2:1 and verse 11. What conduct is unbecoming of a follower of Christ? How does verse 12 say to *conduct [our]selves* instead?

- First Peter 2:17 lists four key responsibilities: *"Honor everyone. Love the brothers and sisters. Fear God. Honor the emperor."* What specific actions could you take this week to live out these instructions?

Though this earth is not our final home and the leaders of this world are not our highest authority, God has placed us here with the purpose and calling to reveal His Kingdom on earth. The way we conduct ourselves in light of this calling speaks volumes to the watching world.

day 25 / MATTHEW 28:18-20; 2 CORINTHIANS 5:18-20

Jesus commanded His disciples to spread the message of salvation and reconciliation to God.

If anything can rally a group of people, it's a common cause and purpose. With a shared target or aim, even the unlikeliest group of people can accomplish great things.

Jesus sent the Holy Spirit to unify and empower His people to fulfill our shared mission: the mandate He gave a few weeks after His resurrection. The task is no small one — and we find it described in our Bible text for today.

Also known as the Great Commission, Matthew 28:18-20 is Jesus' final recorded encounter with His disciples, concluding the Gospel of Matthew. Although this Commission was the last thing He told them before He left the earth, it was certainly no afterthought; in fact, this message is central to why Jesus came to earth.

- What directives did Jesus give His followers in Matthew 28:19-20? How would their obedience to these directives help lead people out of spiritual exile?

Jesus gave His disciples a unifying, communal identity and mission that day. Their lives and expressions of faith were to be marked by action for the sake of the gospel. Evangelism became a primary function of the Church, which existed then — as it exists today and will exist tomorrow — to reunite exiles, inviting the lost to be found through faith in Christ.

In Genesis 1:28, God told Adam and Eve to *"be fruitful, multiply, fill the earth"* with His glory. Though they multiplied physically, sin made it impossible for humans to rightly carry out the spiritual aspect of this calling — because sin is fruitless (Ephesians 5:11) and fills the earth with evil (Jeremiah 46:12). Yet because of who He is and because of His sacrifice, Jesus holds *"all authority"* (Matthew 28:18) to reinstate fallen humans to our rightful rule and reign on earth (Luke 10:19; Colossians 2:10). What sin stripped from us in the garden of Eden, Jesus restored on the cross, ending the exile for those who believe in Him. And not just for a few …

- Look at Matthew 28:19 again. Who did Jesus invite to be part of the family of God?

- Now read 2 Corinthians 5:19. Who is God reconciling to Himself? To whom has He given the rights and privileges of sharing this message of reconciliation?

Both of today's Bible passages reveal the all-encompassing love and outreach of God. God did not send Jesus to save *some people* from a particular place, status or background. Jesus came for *all people* who will believe in and receive Him. Every nation. Every tribe. Every language. The opportunity for reconciliation is open to everyone who will believe. The God who created all people, the One who exiled sinners from Eden and scattered them at the tower of Babel, has sent Jesus to bring His children back into communion with Him.

And because this gift is for all, it is to be proclaimed by all who know Him.

We know Him and make Him known. We strive to be a vibrant community of people becoming more like Christ, sharing the Good News and baptizing believers *"in the name of the Father and of the Son and of the Holy Spirit"* (Matthew 28:19).
- We serve one awesome God who exists in three Persons: Father, Son and Spirit. As we welcome new believers into the Church community, why might it be significant to emphasize the communal nature of God Himself? (For a little extra reading, check out how God revealed Himself as Father, Son and Spirit at Jesus' baptism in Matthew 3:16-17!)

As Dr. Marvin Vincent expounds, "When one is baptized into the name of the Trinity, he professes to acknowledge and appropriate God in all that he is and in all that he does for man. He recognizes and depends upon God the Father as his Creator and Preserver; receives Jesus Christ as his only Mediator and Redeemer, and his pattern of life; and confesses the Holy Spirit as his Sanctifier and Comforter."[38]

What amazing grace that Jesus commissions us – former exiles who have now found forgiveness and belonging in Him – to lead others toward repentance and reconciliation too. That is the Church: the body of Christ.

- Think of a person you know who needs to know our great God. Write a prayer for them below, and consider asking God how you might be instrumental in their salvation.

[38] Vincent, Marvin. *Word Studies in the New Testament,* vol. 1 (New York: Charles Scribner's Sons, 1887), 150.

WEEK 5 WEEKEND *Video* AND *Prayer*

As we conclude Week 5 of our study together, we're excited to share a special video teaching from an expert on this week's topics: our friend Wendy Blight, who serves as Biblical Content Specialist at Proverbs 31 Ministries.

Scan the QR code or visit https://first5.org/video-study to access Wendy's video, where she'll share more insights about this week's scriptures and dig deeper into what we've been learning about exile.

Disclaimer: Links to additional content subject to expiration.

As you watch, feel free to jot down your notes and reflections in the space below — then join us in prayer to wrap up the week.

Father, I come to You with a heart of surrender. I understand the importance of Christ's mission on earth, and I thank You that I am a valuable part of fulfilling His desire to bring wanderers home. Others may reject me, just as they rejected Him. Still, I want to choose to build bridges instead of fences, to prepare tables instead of slamming doors, to stand up for the broken instead of standing up on my soapbox, to lay down my life for others, to be led by Your Spirit and Truth, and to embrace those who feel shunned or ostracized.

Because I belong to You, I belong to the family of God (Psalm 68:6). Thank You that I am no longer alone. I am a living vessel that carries Your presence. I have a purpose and community that can strengthen me in the faith. I praise You for this family You are creating. I will not abandon my brothers and sisters, Your Church, or those who have not yet encountered You.

Show me how to serve You and those around me with humility and grace. Reign over my words. Guide my steps as I follow You. Let my life bring You honor and point others to the cross.

When all is shaken, I know I am safe in You. And though I am not eternally home yet, I am found in You. You've always been my home. You always will be. In Jesus' name, amen.

Where is
our true
home?

WEEK (*Six*)

WHERE IS OUR TRUE HOME?

WEEK SIX

At times, our souls sense a deep longing. Even when we aren't sure exactly what will satisfy that longing … we can't deny that it's there. Throughout our study of exile in the Bible, we've discovered that what we long for most is not something or even someplace — we long for *Someone*. Our hearts long for God and for a time when we won't battle the separation of sin any longer in our relationship with Him.

Ecclesiastes 3:11 says God *"has also put eternity in [our] hearts."* And in our final week together, we will look at the hidden treasure that exile on earth actually presents us: joyful anticipation of God's eternal Kingdom.

First, we will consider in Ephesians 1 the concepts of "already" and "not yet" as they relate to God's Kingdom. According to Scripture, believers are already adopted in Christ (Romans 8:15), but at the same time, we await adoption (Romans 8:23). We are already redeemed in Christ (Ephesians 1:7), but at the same time, there is more redemption to come (Ephesians 4:30). We already have the deposit of our inheritance in Christ through the Holy Spirit (Ephesians 1:13); however, we have not yet realized the full riches to come when our exile on earth is over and we are eternally with God (Ephesians 1:10). When we feel disillusioned by the disappointments of this life, we can thank God for the Holy

Spirit and lean into Him to help us live faithfully in between God's promises and their ultimate fulfillment.

We will also explore Psalm 90 this week, which reminds us that our true home isn't merely a place — our home is in God's presence. He is our dwelling place. In this psalm, Moses called on God in exile, and we can do the same when we are struggling to remember where we belong. We were created to be with God.

And while we wait for Jesus' return, we don't have to sit on our hands. God has purposeful work for us: He doesn't just want us to survive the exile of living as foreigners on earth, but He calls us to thrive. We can accomplish this through His power and walk out an exilic ethic of peace as we live in the tension of being *"citizens of heaven"* (Philippians 1:27) yet dwelling on earth. Dishwashers have to get emptied, emails answered, and meals prepared. But even in the most mundane of earthly tasks, we can pursue godliness.

Finally, while work is important as we seek to flourish in exile, so is rest. God calls us to enter His rest through faith in Christ. If you are feeling weary with any number of heavy burdens, Jesus calls you to come to Him. He wants to carry your load. And in Christ, you can look forward to eternal, perfect rest without the constraints of suffering and sin.

In eternity, we will experience His presence in a way we can't yet wrap our minds around fully. No more death or crying. No more wandering or wilderness. We will know right where we belong each and every day: in a perfect, covenant community of worshippers praising the One who made us, loves us and redeems us.

Now that is a homecoming to look forward to!

— *Melissa Spoelstra*

day 26 / EPHESIANS 1:1-14

The Holy Spirit is the first installment of the Christian's inheritance.

As we come to our final week of studying exile, we've discovered that redemption through Christ ends our spiritual exile and that He created the Church community on earth as a "home away from home" where believers belong together as we await His second coming.

But we've also seen that while we live on this planet, even in the Church, we often ache for heaven. Jesus teaches us to ask the Father for His *will [to] be done on earth as it is in heaven* (Matthew 6:10), and this prayer will come to full fruition in eternity. Until then, we live in the tension of an "already but not yet" Kingdom.

Today we'll study part of a letter the Apostle Paul wrote to the church at Ephesus, encouraging believers to grasp the "already" and live with expectancy of the "not yet." We *already* have the deposit of our inheritance in Christ but *not yet* the full riches of eternity.

· List below at least three spiritual blessings (though there are many more in this passage!) that believers have in Christ **right now,** according to Ephesians 1:3-14:

1.

2.

3.

Paul used a continuous verb tense to reference many blessings in Christ, in essence saying that we have (and are still having) redemption, forgiveness, wisdom, insight and more (vv. 7-8).[39]

We also notice that verse 4 echoes the temple language of the Old Testament with the word *"blameless,"* which once described the sacrificial animals that God's people presented on the altar to cover their sins.[40] For Paul's original readers, mostly Jewish Christians who were familiar with the Old Testament, the concept of *"redemption through [Jesus'] blood"* (v. 7) also would have brought to mind the payment of a ransom price. Christ paid the ransom for our sins with His own blood, fulfilling Leviticus 17:11: *"It is the lifeblood that makes atonement."*

Before Jesus' earthly ministry, God's people brought sacrifices to the temple — but these sacrifices were only temporary, as every new sin required new sacrifice. Today, because of Jesus' self-sacrifice, we can be **forever** *"blameless"* because He *"chose"* and *"adopted"* us (Ephesians 1:4-5)! What was foreshadowed in the sacrificial system was realized at the cross when the Son of God laid down His life for us. And this salvation in Christ includes gentile believers as well as believers from the tribes of Israel who were once exiled and scattered: God *"bring[s] everything together in Christ"* (v. 10).

[39] Frank E. Gaebelein, *The Expositor's Bible Commentary: Ephesians-Philemon,* vol. 11, (Grand Rapids, MI: Zondervan, 1984), 25.

[40] Gaebelein, 25. Note: The word translated *"blameless"* in Genesis 6:9 and *"without blemish"* throughout Leviticus is the same Hebrew word, *tamim.*

- Take a moment to reflect on how your life has changed because you have redemption through Christ. What does it mean for you that you have been adopted into God's family forever?

The blessings of salvation in Christ allow us to live without shame and provide wisdom for daily decisions in our exilic lives. And we know today's blessings are also a foretaste of what is to come. In the phrase translated as *"a plan for the right time"* in Ephesians 1:10, Paul used the Greek word *oikonomia*, which related to household management.[41] God has a far-reaching plan for when His Church's exile will end and heaven will meet earth, fully establishing His Kingdom as our eternal home.

- What further insights do you gain from 1 Corinthians 15:24-28 and Philippians 2:10-11 regarding the end of the Church's exile?

These are details of our future *"inheritance"* (Ephesians 1:11) we haven't yet fully received. While we wait to receive them, Ephesians 1:13-14 assures us of two truths about the Holy Spirit:

1. **The Spirit is a seal:** At the time of Paul's writing, a seal could be attached to a document to certify its authenticity. It could also indicate ownership or represent a title of office. Similarly, the Spirit seals us when we commit ourselves to Christ, guaranteeing the authenticity of our faith, possessing and protecting us, and giving us new titles as sons and daughters of God.

2. **The Spirit is a guarantee:** Paul described the Holy Spirit as a *"down payment"* (v. 14), or guarantee, of our inheritance in Christ. The Greek word for *"down payment"* was borrowed from the commercial world and meant a deposit or first installment assuring a seller that the full amount would eventually follow.[42] This term also applied to engagement rings, which is significant since Jesus calls the Church His bride (Revelation 21:9)!

Friend, today may be hard, but our exile won't last forever. And in the meantime, the Holy Spirit is the first installment of our eternal inheritance. More than just an engagement ring on our finger, He actually lives inside of us — advocating, comforting and guiding us into truth.

- How has the Holy Spirit been active in your life over the course of this study? (For more about the Spirit's ministry, consider John 14:26, Hebrews 10:14-17 and Romans 15:13.)

[41] Gaebelein, 25.
[42] Gaebelein, 25.

day 27 / PSALM 90

God's people find their home in God's presence rather than a place.

Rather than thinking of exile only as a historical event that happened to long-ago people, we now know that "exile is a theological symbol that has developed in powerful and demanding ways far beyond the historicity of [an ancient] time."[43] In other words, exile is powerfully symbolic. We've observed this in many scriptural examples, including the Israelites' displacement in Egypt for 400 years and their 40 years of wandering in the wilderness.

On Days 8-9, we talked about how Moses led God's people out of their Egyptian exile and was with them in the wilderness on their journey to Canaan. But because of his own sin, he never actually entered the promised land himself (see Numbers 20:8-12). And based on today's reading in Psalm 90, written by Moses, we find that exile ultimately gave him clarity to understand that the true home for a follower of God isn't a place so much as it is God Himself.

· What does Psalm 90:1 say the Lord has been *"in every generation"*? How does it comfort and/or convict you to consider that people who were wandering in exile, with no physical place to call home, declared this about God?

· What words or images related to *exile* do you discover in this psalm? What words or images show that to be in God's presence and favor is to be *at home*?

The Hebrew word most often used for *"Lord"* in Psalm 90 is "Adonai." This name comes from the plural form of the Hebrew word *adon*, which means "lord" or "master."[44] In Scripture, individuals often called God "Adonai" when appealing to Him for provision, protection, guidance and care. For instance, Moses also addressed Adonai when he implored God to send someone else to lead His people out of Egypt (Exodus 4:10-13).

---

[43] Walter Brueggemann, *Reverberations of Faith: A Theological Handbook of Old Testament Themes* (Louisville, KY: Westminster John Knox Press, 2002), 70.

[44] Andrew Jukes, *The Names of God: Discovering God as He Desires to Be Known* (Grand Rapids, MI: Kregel Publications, 1967), 111.

When we feel displaced, rejected, desperate or disappointed because this world doesn't feel like home, we can remember it is not our home. Adonai is. The ESV translation of Psalm 90:1 says He is our *"dwelling place."*

We can express our frustrations with exile — Moses did. He described life as *"struggle and sorrow"* (Psalm 90:10). But he also held on to the truth that God is faithful *"from eternity to eternity"* (Psalm 90:2). We can live in this tension as well: holding the heartache of exile in tandem with the hope of a heavenly home.

· According to verse 12, what should a person do to gain a heart of wisdom during our time on earth?

· Take a moment right now to ask God to teach you to do the same. Jot a brief prayer below:

Spiritually, our exile ends when we trust in Christ, who reconciles us back to the Father and gives us His Spirit so we are never alone or lost again. Physically, our exile on earth will continue until the day when all believers dwell with God in the perfection of a restored, eternal Eden, without sin's toil and trouble affecting our relationship with Him. In the meantime, we can number our days and say with Moses, *"Return, O Lord!"* (v. 13, ESV). We can dwell in Him, rather than a place, as our true home.

day 28 / 2 PETER 3:1-13

Peter called believers to live holy lives as we wait for the new heaven and the new earth.

Even when we know God's promises, sometimes we struggle to find purpose in the pain we experience. The longer it takes for God's promises to be fulfilled, the more time we have to doubt whether they will ever come to fruition.

That's why the Apostle Peter wrote a letter to the Church to remind believers that **Jesus will return.** The exile ethic of the Church therefore does not involve sitting in misery but living with holy hope, rejoicing in the present blessings of salvation in Christ and anticipating the bright future to come. It can be tempting just to focus on surviving the toil and trouble of this world ... but God actually calls us to thrive in the midst of it.

- In 2 Peter 3:2, whose *"words previously spoken"* and whose *"command"* did Peter ask believers to remember? (Note: An "apostle" in the New Testament was someone personally called and commissioned by Jesus to spread the gospel, like Peter or Paul.)

- How might this idea of remembering the past relate to our own study of exile throughout God's Scriptures?

First, Peter urges us to remember the prophets: for instance, Jeremiah and Daniel, who both prophesied during the time of the Judean exile to Babylon. Both of these prophets give us some insight into how to live faithfully for God even while in exile.

- Read Jeremiah 29:4-7. What were God's people called to build? To plant? To find?

God's people in exile were to seek the welfare of the city where they were living. Yes, the welfare of Babylon: a pagan land where they were being held captive!

God's calling for His people in this passage also mirrors the calling He gave in the garden of Eden, encouraging the first humans to be fruitful and multiply. In the midst of our exile, we, too, can recall Eden, and we can ask the Father for His will to be done on earth as it is in heaven (Matthew 6:10). The triad of home, garden and family reminds us of our peaceful ethic as exiles and hints at the tranquility of Eden that will be restored in eternity.

Additionally, the prophet Daniel gives us another example of how to engage in limited cooperation with a foreign land while also maintaining spiritual integrity. Daniel took a Babylonian name and wore Babylonian clothes, but he drew clear boundaries to prioritize his allegiance to God's Kingdom over allegiance to any earthly king.

- For instance, Daniel served the pagan King Darius during his reign, but when Darius' government outlawed prayer, what did Daniel do? Read the story in Daniel 6:10-13 and summarize below:

- How does Daniel's example help us understand *"what sort of people [we] should be in holy conduct and godliness,"* as 2 Peter 3:11 describes?

As a wisdom warrior, Daniel learned to be loyal above all to God. In the same way, we live as a community of faith in a world that is often indifferent, and at times hostile, to the gospel. But we persist in leading righteous lives and loving others in Jesus' name because He *"is patient … not wanting any to perish but all to come to repentance"* (2 Peter 3:9).

Peter wanted his readers in the Church to know how to live while we wait for exile to end. He said our lives are to be characterized by holiness and godliness because *"based on [God's] promise, we wait for new heavens and a new earth, where righteousness dwells"* (2 Peter 3:13). This means not just living for today but living with the end in mind.

- How is the Lord encouraging you toward holiness and godliness in your life this week?

We can't live holy lives without the Holy Spirit, even if we "try harder" to "do better." That's why Peter didn't shame his readers in light of *"the day of God"* (v. 12) but rather cast a vision of the new heaven and new earth that emphasized God's patience and kindness in waiting for people to repent. We can learn from this to be gentle with ourselves, too, even as we ask the Lord to renew our minds with thoughts of His coming. By His power, you and I can grow in godliness as we wait.

day 29 / HEBREWS 4

God offers rest to His people.

If we could sum up the seasons of exile we've looked at throughout this study, "restful" wouldn't likely be the word we would use. In fact, the people who were exiled in Egypt, Assyria and Babylon might have used words like "tired" or "weary" in conversations surrounding their long journeys, building projects, replanting of gardens, and acclimating to new customs and rules.

Our lives can sometimes feel exhausting as well. Yet God offers us rest. For Christians, this rest comes to us right now — and also foreshadows a greater rest to come.
   · Read Hebrews 4:1-10, and write below any words or phrases associated with being able to enter God's rest:

Did you notice how words like *"faith"* and *"believed"* are connected to rest? The writer of Hebrews in the New Testament recalled the wilderness wanderers in the Old Testament who could not enter God's promised land because of their unbelief, complaining, idolatry and rebellion against God (Hebrews 3:16-19). But he pointed out that although these ancient Israelites did not enter God's rest, *"the promise to enter his rest remains"* (Hebrews 4:1).

So who will receive the fulfillment of this promise? Verse 3 tells us: *"we who have believed"* in Jesus.

Hebrews 4:9 is no longer speaking of Canaan as the promised land of rest but rather a new, eternal promised land of rest. Furthermore, the *"Sabbath rest [that] remains for God's people"* (v. 9) isn't a state of complacency but rather a state of contented trust that God has done the work of forgiveness through the offering of His Son. Sabbath rest isn't just the absence of work. Hebrews 4:10 even references the creation account and how God rested on the seventh day, having finished the work of creation (Genesis 2:2) — but He didn't enter a state of idleness.
   · What does John 5:17 reveal to us about both the Father and the Son?

You may have heard the song "Working for the Weekend." Even if you haven't, you might understand that sentiment: On earth, it often feels like we're working just to be able to rest. And God created us knowing we need rest. But the Sabbath pattern He instituted for His people in Genesis 2:2 wasn't just about resting *from work*. Rest also gives us the energy we need *for work*, so that we *"do not grow weary in doing good"* (2 Thessalonians 3:13). As believers, we both work and rest for God's glory, our joy and the joy of others.

- What else do you learn about Sabbath in Exodus 31:13 and Ezekiel 20:20? What is it meant to signify or teach us?

- Have you ever envisioned eternity as a realm where you might get bored or have nothing to do? How does today's study change your perspective on eternal rest as purposeful rather than merely passive?

Today, believers in Christ can work out our salvation **from** a place of rest because Christ has done the work **for** our salvation: *"It is God who is working in [us] both to will and to work according to his good purpose"* (Philippians 2:13). On the cross, Jesus offered Himself as the perfect sacrifice for our sin. He now calls us to come to Him for rest.

Finally, it's interesting to note that where Hebrews 4:8 mentions Joshua's attempt to lead God's people toward rest in the Old Testament, the original audience would have noticed a play on words: "Joshua" is the Hebrew form of the Greek name "Jesus." In essence, "There had been a 'Jesus' who could not lead his people into the rest of God just as there was another 'Jesus' who could."[45]

- Read Matthew 11:28-30, and write below what Jesus asks us to do to receive His rest:

On earth, Jesus offers us a foretaste of the rest that the end of our exile will bring. Revelation 14:13 speaks of an ultimate rest we will experience in Christ: *"Then I heard a voice from heaven saying, 'Write: Blessed are the dead who die in the Lord from now on.' 'Yes,' says the Spirit, 'so they will rest from their labors, since their works follow them.'"*

Hebrews 4:16 also gives us an image of standing before God's throne, which we will do someday in eternity. At the same time, *"let us approach"* is a call to draw near to Jesus today, right now! Coming to God's throne of grace with faith and expectation is the pathway to present and future rest.

[45] Frank E. Gaebelein, *The Expositor's Bible Commentary: Hebrews-Revelation*, vol. 12, (Grand Rapids, MI: Zondervan, 1984), 42.

Take a moment now to pause and come to God's throne in prayer. Below, express your sources of weariness, confess any areas of disobedience, and thank God for the mercy and grace you find in His presence:

day 30 / REVELATION 21

A new heaven and a new earth will mark the end of exile.

As we come to this last day of our study together, our feelings might be a little bittersweet. Looking at the concept of exile in the Bible can feel both encouraging and discouraging at the same time. Realizing we are aliens and strangers who will never feel a perfect sense of belonging on earth in its current state can be unsettling; however, it is comforting to normalize the idea that our fallen world is not supposed to be this way. We were meant to live in perfect union with our Creator. Once we've seen this thread of exile throughout the biblical text and our own lives, we can't unsee it.

· Take a moment to reflect on all you've learned about exile in this Bible study. Record a few insights that have stood out to you, and/or a few questions you still have, below:

We are wanderers longing for homecoming. Thankfully, in Christ, we have much to look forward to in the future. The union with God that Adam and Eve enjoyed in Eden before sin entered the world will be restored when God gives us a new heaven and a new earth. In fact, the new heaven and new earth will be even greater than Eden. Bible teacher Nancy Guthrie writes, "Evil made its way into Eden and brought ruin with it. The new creation, where we will make our home forever, will be completely secure."[46] While every believer in Christ *has been saved* from the penalty of sin and *is being saved* from the power of sin, in eternity we *will be saved* from the very presence of and potential for sin.

· Revelation 21 offers some amazingly vivid prophecies of what our eternal home will be like. What are some of the images associated with the new heaven and new earth?

· What will *not* be included in this new heaven and earth (vv. 4, 8, 22-23, 27)?

In Revelation 21, we encounter many allusions to the Old Testament and the garden of Eden. The parallels between Revelation 21 and Genesis 1-2 (before the first sin) include: the absence of death and suffering, God dwelling with people, the tree of life, and the absence of a curse.

[46] Nancy Guthrie, "Heaven Will Be Better Than Eden," Desiring God, September 1, 2018, https://www.desiringgod.org/articles/heaven-will-be-better-than-eden.

Yet Revelation 21 also repeatedly emphasizes that our eternal home will be *"new"* (vv. 1-2, 5) — not merely another Eden but someplace better. The Greek word for "new" (*kaine*) means "new in quality, fresh, rather than recent or new in time (*neos*)."[47] What makes it new is that God will be there dwelling with us more personally, tangibly and intimately than ever before. Our true sense of belonging will be fully realized as we will be together with God and our forever family of brothers and sisters who are loyal to Him.

Heaven is a place that culture at times depicts with clouds, harps and inactivity. But Revelation 21 reminds us that our future includes life, activity, interest and people. No boring clouds or harps here!

Scholar N.T. Wright reminds us that eternity isn't just about believers going up to heaven but about heaven coming down to earth: "In Scripture from start to finish we are taught that heaven and earth belong together; that the Creator's purpose always was to bring together all things in heaven and on earth in the Messiah (Eph 1:10); that the final scene, as in Revelation 21, will not be saved souls going up to heaven but the New Jerusalem coming down from heaven to earth."[48]

- John, the writer of Revelation, isn't the only biblical writer who spoke about a new heaven and a new earth. How does Isaiah 65:17-25 overlap with Revelation 21, and what parallels and unique details about eternity stand out to you in these passages?
    - Parallels:

    - Unique details:

All of these truths about the future lead us to live today in light of what is coming. God's Word gives us hope that all He has promised us will actually be fulfilled. Exile has an expiration date. Even if we feel like we don't belong right now — in our neighborhood, workplace, friend group, church or even our family — **we belong with God both today and forever.**

- As you think about the new heaven and the new earth, what specific encouragement can you take to heart today?

[47] Frank E. Gaebelein, *The Expositor's Bible Commentary: Hebrews-Revelation*, vol. 12, (Grand Rapids, MI: Zondervan, 1984), 592.
[48] James M. Scott, *Exile: A Conversation with N.T. Wright* (Downers Grove, IL: IVP Academic, 2017), 321.

WEEK 6 WEEKEND *Video* AND *Prayer*

As we conclude the final week of our study, we're excited to share a special closing video message from the writer of this week's study, Melissa Spoelstra.

Scan the QR code or visit https://first5.org/video-study to access Melissa's video, where she'll share more insights about this week's scriptures and dig deeper into what we've been learning about exile.

Disclaimer: Links to additional content subject to expiration.

As you watch, feel free to jot down your notes and reflections in the space below — then join us in prayer to wrap up the week.

Lord, thank You for helping us learn more about exile from Genesis to Revelation. Continue to give us eyes to see how You are working in us and all around us. We can't wait for the day when heaven comes down to earth and You make all things new! Until then, show us what it looks like to thrive — even when it feels like we are living in Babylon or wandering in a wilderness. Lord, we pray for the peace of the land of our exile. Show us how we can contribute to its welfare and share Your gospel message with those who are far from You, that You may bring them home to the new heaven and earth in eternity. In Jesus' name, amen.

NOTES

NOTES

NOTES

NOTES

READY FOR YOUR NEXT STUDY?

1 & 2 Timothy: The Clarity You Need When Life Feels Chaotic, Confusing and out of Control